Letters from an
EXTREME PILGRIM

Letters from an
EXTREME PILGRIM

Reflections on Life, Love and the Soul

Peter Owen Jones

RIDER

London • Sydney • Auckland • Johannesburg

1 3 5 7 9 10 8 6 4 2

First published in 2010 by Rider Books, an imprint of Ebury Publishing
A Random House Group Company

The Random House Group Limited Reg. No. 954009

Addresses for companies within the Random House Group can be found at
www.randomhouse.co.uk

A CIP catalogue record for this book is available from the British Library

The Random House Group Limited supports The Forest Stewardship Council (FSC),
the leading international forest certification organisation. All our titles that are printed
on Greenpeace approved FSC certified paper carry the FSC logo. Our paper procurement
policy can be found at www.rbooks.co.uk/environment

Mixed Sources
Product group from well-managed
forests and other controlled sources
www.fsc.org Cert no. TT-COC-2139
© 1996 Forest Stewardship Council

FSC

Printed and bound in the UK by
CPI Mackays, Chatham ME5 8TD

ISBN 9781846041334

To buy books by your favourite authors and register for offers visit

**KENT LIBRARIES
AND ARCHIVES**

For my mothers

Contents

Acknowledgements

My thanks must go to one Father Lazarus, who very
kindly lent me his cave to stay in: I have, as you
advised, taken some of the desert home with me.
Thank you for giving it to me.

And to Graham Jonson,
who dropped the food off.

Preface

I have been fortunate enough to be able to experience a long-held dream. Early one summer, I spent some time on a life-changing retreat, during which I was thrust into a cave up in the mountains above St Anthony's Monastery in Egypt, where I was instructed to live a very strict life of prayer, eating only one full meal a day. I have no idea why I should have wanted to be – and, to a certain extent, still crave to be – in a desert environment. As places, deserts test us in every way; there is something so utterly uncompromising about the landscape that, in time, illusion has to wither.

The cave in which I lived was a small crevice between two rock faces in the eastern Sinai Desert in Egypt. It was (and still is) the hermitage of Father Lazarus, a Coptic hermit who has lived there for the last eight years. The accommodation was basic: no bed – just my sleeping bag on the floor, a tiny desk, a kitchen the size of a cupboard and a few small icons balanced in crevices in the rocks. Outside there was a terrace and an area of shade.

In the morning, prayers started at five and continued every three hours throughout the day, with each prayer session lasting forty-five minutes. Breakfast consisted of nuts and a little dried fruit, lunch was rice and maybe a tomato, and the evening meal was more nuts and fruit. I had plenty of time in which to think.

Just before I left to go on the retreat, the idea of writing letters to the people and entities who have shaped my being came into focus. So here they are, in this book. It has sadly not been possible to include one of the original letters written in the cave, but two have been added since my return to England.

In the process of writing these letters, I have had the opportunity to think about the nature of relationships. Our relationship with God is perhaps formed when we are very young. When we are growing up there are so many doorways into new worlds, which feel as if they have just been made. They have. Everything is continually being made anew and whilst we cannot express this ourselves as children, we can perceive this newness far better than adults do – perhaps because we are experiencing so many things for the first time. When, as adults, we leave our familiar surroundings, as I did in going to the Sinai Desert, we may become more aware of the completeness of this moment and, once we become aware of this, we can perhaps begin to see everything as it really is: life in its state of constant renewal. And when we can sense this, we can begin to feel ourselves in that fluid state of constant renewal, of continual creation. When we become aware of ourselves in such a place something changes in us; something is found. When we can see the world as new, we are perhaps closer to the reality of the divine, who is there in the present moment, literally *being* creation.

Neither I nor anyone else will ever prove the existence of God, because God is not a separate entity; God is a state of being. God is the song thrush on my bird table, not the 'meaning' of the song thrush on my bird table. The notion of proving the existence of God looks increasingly ludicrous to me, as does the notion of disproving it. Western Christianity has been held captive by an empirical quest and has essentially become lost in its quest for proof, where no proof is needed. We are currently being held to ransom by all the dances we call theologies and consequently we are prisoners in the very prison we have built: Christianity has become imprisoned in our minds. What Jesus taught was consciousness; He taught *being*, being in the gaze of God, being aware of the oneness of all life. He doesn't speak to the mind, He speaks to the soul.

While the Church continues to trudge towards awakening, at the moment there seems to be an increasing awareness that humankind is set for great change spiritually. This will probably involve an untying of ourselves from so many of the narratives that have been pretty much imposed upon us, and a learning that we can in fact see with many different eyes and inhabit many different states of being. This is what is meant by the notions of 'being as one', 'being at one with'. We cannot truly love our enemies unless we are willing to 'be at one' with them.

The narrative of our relationship with the divine has been informed over millennia by men and women who have taken themselves out of the swim and placed themselves alone in the wilderness to spend some time with whom they imagined God to be. They ventured inwards, navigating to the furthest shores of their being, which is our being as well. If you think about it, it's a very strange thing to do. I can only say that theirs is a calling; they are called to live in these places, called to exist in this way. Such a calling is a request we can choose to respond to and, in so doing, far from opting out we are in fact opting in. Many of the world religions began with men and women alone in this way, alone in caves, alone in deserts.

Being alone in the desert gave rise to these letters, written to some of those who have made me who I am.

Dear Joan,

Firstly, thank you, thank you for giving me life, for each moment – for this moment. I want you to know I love being alive; just the sheer *being* of it, the delight and the pain. I am not sure parents should protect their children from pain – it is as inevitable as morning – although maybe we should teach our children how to deal with it. Growing up without you was at times hard because I felt different, as if I had a secret. No matter how often I told the secret (and I was always very open about the fact I was adopted), nothing seemed to take root in that place where you would have been. It was at times like living with hunger.

So I invented you. I invented queens and Amazons, I invented someone who could see me from far away; someone who understood and forgave; whose affection was unquestioned, whose affection belonged to me. I made up stories too: like the time when you appeared in Tunbridge High Street once and you got out of a Jaguar in your white stilettos and that white dress with red spots; I never saw your eyes because you were wearing sunglasses and the sun was shining. But no matter how much I invented you, you were never there.

Once I remember being on a canal boat on the Thames. I was with Jacs, Quentin and Sally. We came round a bend on the river and there was this house just beneath the brow of a hill; it came to me that I had been there before and I knew instantly the tiles in the hallway, the carpet on the stairs, how the oak was polished, the sound of footsteps above. You were there, or you and I had been there, or I had been there inside you – I had ingested it all.

You should know that girls loved you. To Felicity, you were a countess who had an affair with the Irish stable boy. Katie was certain you were musical – more likely than not a violinist – and that you had been seduced by a long-haired Norwegian conductor. Jo, who was always very practical when it came to dreams, reckoned you probably worked for a medium-sized company as a typist. One night you understandably drank too much and allowed a colleague into your bed. Jo imagined that you hadn't told the person what had happened; that you simply handed in your notice and left when you discovered you were pregnant.

I have to say most of my male friends thought you were a scullery maid who had succumbed to the charms of an Irish stable lad who put himself about a bit, or his lordship, who was of course married at the time. No one predicted that you were studying for an MA in Economics and History at St Andrews University, where you fell in with the dashing but dangerous medical students, one of whom clearly did not fully comprehend the reality that when a sperm penetrates an egg it is a beginning as well as a guaranteed end. None of them assumed my grandfather would have been the proprietor of a small hotel overlooking St Andrews golf course.

I am so glad you kept some of my grandfather's letters. I especially liked the one in which he tells you that he has bought a new carpet for the guests' drawing room. I loved hearing about the time you drove round Scotland together while he sat there in the passenger seat smoking his pipe, with his dog on a tartan blanket on his lap. You say I am like him, that I look like him albeit without the kilt; my hands are his hands and there is that twinkle. I am glad he had a twinkle in his eye, or maybe it was just when you were around.

You know, I never felt remotely Scottish. But something truly happens inside me whenever I am near streams and bracken, where I begin to feel I belong. The closest I came to this as a child was in Ashdown Forest and later, as a man, the same feelings of real belonging returned whenever I was in mountains – that mixture of water, bilberries and stone, all that gold in the grass.

When Jacs and I were married we had a house in London where the council were giving out grants for roof and bathroom repairs. We ended up with an Irish builder, who turned up just after eleven, took to the pub at twelve, wobbled back at half past three, then banged in a couple of nails and knocked off at four. He managed to convince me I had a 'Sherkin face'. Apparently there is a race of people who all look like me living on Sherkin Island off the coast of County Cork. Then there was the time Alan took me to meet a photographer's assistant in the Dog and Duck in Soho. I had been sceptical and little churlish with Alan about the fact that I had a spitting image, but there he was, sitting in front of me in the pub. First, the photographer's assistant drank far too much beer far too quickly; then he set about eating the daffodils on the table. Half an hour after that he started throwing up outside. Sadly I haven't seen him since.

Only once did anyone say anything cruel about you. It was in chapel at the public school I was unfortunate enough to attend. The headmaster stood up and said that adopted children were always going to be slightly unbalanced, implying they came from an unreliable source. I am firmly of the opinion now that being adopted is actually a blessing, not a curse. Moreover, there is nothing more unbalanced than a grown man beating a small boy with a bamboo cane in order to assert control and any opinions that such a man might proffer should be treated with nothing other than mild amusement. But what he said hurt all the more because at the time it cut through the theatre of invention I had built around myself, into a place that was forever lonely and cut off from others.

Whilst it fosters self-reliance, such a lonely space does so by quelling emotions. It meant that whilst physically I was able to take the bamboo beatings, I was never going to give the headmaster the satisfaction of crying. The tears I was determined to hold back were not in response to the physical pain; they were more of an emotional response that somebody could be so cold and so cruel. That was a reason worth crying for, but I never did, not until I was much older.

I gathered images of fields and butterflies, of bedrooms, pools and other safe places, and I projected them onto the surface of that lonely space. But in time my reality became an endless reel of films, which I was watching; until one day that was all there was – nothing but celluloid, no connection at all. The first psychotherapist I saw, well, we just talked, I don't even remember what about. You see, I had notions about what I really loved even then, but I had also invented so much of myself because I didn't know *who* I was; this 'I' was so many people. Anyway, it must have been towards the end of our conversation that the psychotherapist looked at me and said, 'You have a very lonely core,' and I broke down at that point with relief, almost joy, because she had seen the truth and I was at last able to acknowledge it, to accept your utter absence.

Just before that meeting I had tried to find you. After a

brief interview at the records house, St Catherine's House, I was given a yellow piece of paper with my name on it: the name you had given me. The paper also had your name on it, which led me to believe I was Irish, that my namesake was a brand of whisky. But that was as far as I got. I burnt the scrap of paper on the roof of the West End building I was working in at the time.

The psychotherapy really helped. It enabled me to accept that the space inside me was just a space and helped me to de-clutter it of the creations – the rewards, excuses and a few jewels – that my imagination had filled it with over the years, from the time I was seven years old. It became wholesome rather than empty.

One thing I do wish was that Daphne had kept the note that you had written to her when you handed me over for adoption. You gave her some towels and some baby clothes as well, but she threw them away and I understand why: not because she is mean or unfeeling but because she needed to begin from zero. I just would like to have seen that note, that's all.

I remember watching Jacs with our own children when they were very young, when they were babies. She was so beautiful with them, fierce and loving, with a love that males can only receive; we cannot give. I knew that with each gift of a child I would see you; there would be a glimpse of you. There would be mannerisms, the shapes of hands and eyes, and all that curly hair that Jonnie has – red as the Cuillin hills.

After Eden was born Al's brother Mike said he would download my original birth certificate from the web. I knew people who had been looking for years for their mothers and so I didn't expect to find you after just one call to directory enquiries, followed by one call to the hotel, who put me on to your brother.

Thank you for flying over from Canada after we spoke on the phone for the first time and for sending all those pictures. I really liked the one of you as a girl in your kilt, your knees all dirty, holding that lamb in your arms. We were both so nervous meeting on the platform of St Andrews station. You handled it beautifully although you did stare a lot at first. Then you started cracking jokes with the taxi driver. We sat in the hotel overlooking the golf course, drinking tea and eating expensive biscuits. I think the new owners had replaced the carpet, and you told me about butchers on the Isle of Man, about art dealers in Edinburgh and pubs in the Lake District. There were some darknesses as well; I really admired you for speaking about them.

My brothers came as a big surprise, literally – six foot one and six foot two tall – and an even bigger surprise was that you had married my father. I still don't really understand why you did that, although I can understand why you separated. But I have this horrible feeling that you married to justify me; to somehow put the stamp of love on my birth, to make everyone feel better. It was an act of healing that perhaps you both needed at the time and whilst I *might* have been the glue – and it is a *might* – I fear that glue turned into a ghost. I could sense that when I came to visit you in Canada. A ghost that stood at every turning that wasn't taken. And whilst you were both old enough to make your own decisions – and however well intentioned your decision was to get married at the time – I was in so many ways what became the empty space between you.

I can't say I really enjoyed west coast Canadian architecture, but I really enjoyed David's house tucked into the forest with the river chuckling nearby. I enjoyed our time together and I loved being with my brothers. I was taken by the oil picture above the fireplace of my grandfather as a boy and your comfortable house with the blue jays on the decking.

I am constantly amazed that you are there, real and laughing. I never for one second felt angry about being put up for adoption. The more we speak the more grateful I am that you endured the social ignominy of the day and survived those months in London whilst I was growing inside you. Thank you for breastfeeding me; I know you said it was against the rules at that home for unmarried mothers in South London. But you and I have never excelled at sticking to the rules; it must be in the blood.

Thank you for telling me you love me – I know you always have, and I you.

Peter

Dear Daddy,

I don't think I would have called you by any other name when I was little – not 'Dad', not Alan. I was only four years old when you died; I don't remember ever addressing you at all. I don't even remember you holding me.

I don't remember your eyes or your hands, but I can see you driving past the front gate of the house. I can see you there now, at the wheel of your grey Morris Minor. You must have been on your way back to the surgery after doing some house calls. You waved and smiled as you drove past.

I can also see you sprinkling talcum powder on the wooden floor in the dining room. It was the morning after you and Daphne had had a party, and the table and the chairs were gone. I think you were dancing the Charleston that morning and you were wearing stripy pyjamas.

Thank you for the Indian headdress and the kaleidoscope you put in my Christmas stocking. I loved them both; I can still remember that first journey into the kaleidoscope, the sound it made, like the sea on a pebbled beach, as the pieces of plastic tumbled into place.

Thank you too for coming into my bedroom three weeks before you died. You sat down in the doorway and I pushed a toy car across the lino to you. As you pushed it back you collapsed and lay there not moving, while Daphne rushed up the stairs. I don't think she was pleased you were out of bed, although I'm sure you were wearing a shirt and tie; but maybe not.

I wasn't aware how much effort it must have taken you to raise your arm to wave goodbye. It must have been the day you were finally moved into the hospital, when a doctor asked if you knew how serious your condition was. Many years later Daphne said you had been working too hard – too many early mornings, too many late nights. When you collapsed at a drinks party no one knew you only had five weeks to live, that the point where your spinal cord meets your brain had become swollen and inflamed, and that in time it would paralyse you.

Daphne has never spoken about your death. Well, to be fair I've never asked her about the details; I didn't want to take her back to that morning. You see, being a child, it really wasn't that painful for me, wasn't painful at all. But Daphne told us beautifully. S and I had just got up; we were playing in my bedroom when she came in. I remember she was wearing a short white nightie; she sat us down on my bed, then sat between us and said: 'I have something terribly sad to tell you. Daddy died last night.' I didn't cry and neither did S, but I knew Daphne had been crying. She seemed so unsteady when she left the room; it was as if she had to leave to go back to her bedroom to cry alone.

When you died you were front-page news in the local paper. You had a quarter of a column in the *Daily Telegraph*, where the headline simply read: 'Brilliant young doctor dies'. After that, whenever I went down the High Street with my bike a steady stream of strangers would emerge and come up to me to tell me what a wonderful man you were. To begin with, when I was very little, the women would kneel down to speak to me. I remember one of them had tears in her eyes. Some of them would hold me, but I didn't understand. Now I'm sure they were imagining losing their own young husbands and having to tell their small children.

Your dying left a huge hole in our lives. I found out many years later that on the day you died, you and Daphne had been due to collect another baby boy from the adoption centre; that you had planned to adopt a total of four children. I am sorry you and Daphne never met the other two and that you didn't get to move into that big house with high hedges up near the end of the village like you'd once planned to do. I used to bicycle past it and I'd tell all my friends, the ones who lived in big houses, that I too was going to live in a big house.

I'm so glad you liked jazz; I enjoy it more and more these days. I love that picture of you wearing a dress suit with a top hat, a fag in your mouth and a row of cards in your hand – you looked great.

I'm afraid I wasn't much help to Daphne after you'd gone; in fact, I was more of a pain in the arse than anything else. I think I did some gardening once in a while, for which she gave me sixpence. It can't have been easy for her – back in the sixties single-parent families with young children were a rarity.

It wasn't until I became a teenager that you appeared again. It was then that I realised I couldn't relate to men at all. After you died the men in my life were mainly teachers, but they were figures of authority rather than of love or tenderness. With a few notable exceptions I began to feel nothing other than disdain for most of them. I could almost hear what they were thinking: that it was hardly surprising I behaved the way I did. After all, I didn't have a father to discipline me.

It is only since I have been fortunate enough to have children of my own that I have been taught that fatherhood is an essential expression of male love, and that this love is fundamental to learning what makes a man, or what a man can be. In my usual haphazard fashion, for many years I thought being a father was something that could be slotted in around being a husband, being a gardener, around earning a living. It wasn't until your first granddaughter was about three years old that I realised being a father was something separate: it is a love all of its own. Once that happened, I started to notice men as fathers and how beautiful their children made them.

Your own father was wonderful; he was all garden

implements and bicycle clips, deaf as a post in his old age. He would walk around the flat he shared with your mother in Swanage and assume that because he could no longer hear himself breaking wind nobody else could either. Your mother was the most gentle human being I have ever met in my life; I never heard her raise her voice and she left nothing other than warmth and affection behind her. Her gift is that she generates those feelings still. To this day I feel terrible that I didn't write to your father to tell him how sorry I was when she died of angina.

After your death we would visit your parents once a year, usually in the spring holidays. Daphne would pack S and me off to Swanage for a week where we would catch buses here and there, or walk along the beach and then back up those red lino stairs to their top-floor flat. Your mother made the best mashed potatoes I've ever eaten – I don't know how she did it – and your father continued his bicycling hobby, going up and down from Land's End to John o'Groats. I think he had made the journey sixteen times by the time he moved to Australia to live with your brother.

It wasn't until I went to theological college that I had any inkling about what being a Quaker meant: that your mother and father had sought to understand and feel God in the silence waiting for us on the inside; that they believed there is no need for churches, priests, hymns, bread and wine; that God will speak and does speak in us and through us when we go to meet with Him/Her in this great silence.

A couple of years ago I was invited to take a funeral for a Quaker family who had chosen a woodland burial. When they needed somewhere to meet beforehand, I offered them the use of the church in Harlton, where they sat together in the choir stalls. Occasionally someone stood up and said something next to the open coffin. It was one of the most honest funerals I have ever attended, certainly one of the most relaxed; there was a simplicity and a true grace about it. It wasn't that there were no formalities – what struck me was that there was just no need of them; that we have perhaps made God into something formal, when in fact God is natural, utterly natural, as natural as breathing. Anyway, I looked at their faces and I understood then where your mother and father were coming from. For the first time, it was as if I knew them as an adult, not as a child: there was all that natural kindness and grace your mother had, as well as the diligent practicality of your father, never

Dear David,

I have no idea how I would have addressed you as a child. Would it have been Mr Bartleet, Revd Bartleet? – I don't know. The last time I heard about you before you died was at S's wedding. Daphne said she had asked you to take it, to officiate, but I think you were a bishop by then and you couldn't, or else the dates were mixed up

I went to Sheila's funeral the other day. I'm sure you would have known her – she lived with John just out on the edge of Staffhurst Wood. Your name came up at her wake, where someone mentioned how you had garnered all the young married couples around you in the hopes of bringing the church to life. I was slightly shocked to hear that. In fact, on reflection I was perturbed to hear you had been made Bishop; colourless company men most of them, although

19

there are of course some notable exceptions. I never saw you in that light and, being a priest now, it is hard for me to imagine you in that company.

Maybe I have always retained a childish view of you as a man, seen through the eyes of the child that I was? As a child, I found you to be nothing other than extraordinary. You were different, so very different from the men who wore suits and who would turn up with their wives for drinks parties at our home in Oak Tree House. Among them there were commuters to London, solicitors, merchant bankers, but there was also a farmer whom I loved from the first moment I met him. He was like you but nothing like you; he was different too.

Was it your hands? Daphne said you had healing hands and she spoke those words quietly when she said them. She became softer when she talked of you, as if you had left some stillness within her, a part of yourself. You were so very still, not in the sense that you didn't move, but in how your very being radiated stillness.

I don't recall one conversation we had; I don't even remember you speaking to me. Yet you must have done, because I can see the room in your house where you taught me how to set butterflies. A board with a groove down the middle, little strips of paper and pins. Your vicarage backed onto some fields where your son and I would hang out. He was brave, your son; I knew he was adopted, like me. Once, when we must have been about eleven years old and we found a starling's nest in some garden sheds, I asked him if he had ever seen you naked and he said he hadn't. I think you became more mysterious then; I wondered whether you were the one unable to have children.

I'm sure there was a clay bust in your study that you were working on, but I'm not sure if it was ever fired or not. In church on Easter Sunday, there were these little cards on the pews which asked the congregation to give generously as on that day the collection went directly to you. That has all been stopped now – for tax reasons. I remember hoping that Daphne would put some extra money inside the collection bags.

Why? Why this focus on you? You had a different engine, or you were powered on a different fuel – and somehow I understood; I just knew that who and what you were was a result of your relationship with God. You were gentle because of your relationship with God; you were kind, you were still. Most of the other men were on the make. They were chancers, although there's nothing wrong with that really. I could see their cars were important to them but I had the feeling that your car wasn't important to you at all – what make, what colour really didn't matter to you.

When we had all these dreary Old Testament readings at school there was always a mention of someone who was 'a man of God' or someone 'on whom God's favour rested'. Because it was all such a long time ago and they all owned camels or were shepherd boys, the 'man of God' meant nothing to me at first. But it all became perfectly clear when I thought of you and your yearning and thirsting after righteousness. You were who we could become if we did the same, and I knew instinctively that it was good.

Such goodness didn't mean following the rules; it meant following goodness, experiencing goodness so that you *became* goodness. With your example, goodness wasn't just something I had to be, or that I had to be coerced into being; it was something I could choose like you had chosen it. You radiated it and I knew you could be trusted to be fair – unlike the men in suits; that you could be trusted to act in the best interests of others, even if the outcome wasn't necessarily something you wanted. The concept of justice, the fundamental nature of justice, is so highly attuned in children and it was something you gave me confidence in: that justice really did exist and there were human beings who were prepared to uphold justice and who would not let it be compromised by self-interest.

Not having a father meant that in the main I observed men rather than got to know them, and the more I observed them the less I trusted them. I would watch them dancing with each other's wives, watch their eyes saying *sleep with me, sleep with me*. I never saw you dancing; maybe you had no need of it. So I could be like them or I could be like you. Too much of my life I have spent trying to be like you, whilst behaving like them.

Righteousness is a very unfashionable word. It has become a faded concept, something that belongs to biblical figures. We understand it, admire it perhaps, but we think we don't need it any more; it is like an old wooden-handled scythe, shaped and dented through reaping, and now we don't reap any more. No – righteousness belongs to King David maybe. Secularism has completely obliterated the persona of the 'righteous man' or the righteous woman. The few that are left on the planet have perhaps fled into the hills, where I am now – but I am not one of them.

You to me embodied righteousness, it shone out of you. I could see it in you as a child and it was so strong, so graceful, so just. You had allowed yourself, I think, to be shaped by God through prayer and God became alive in you – as a child I could see that. Now I can sense it, but I can't necessarily see it any more.

Your influence went very deep. You were a deep seed: sometimes you made flowers and sometimes you made thorns; both grow along the pathways of righteousness.

Dear Desmond,

I wish I could have posted this to you six months ago, as sadly you're no longer around to read it. I know you wanted to die, or maybe a better way of putting it would be that you were ready to die. I loved the way that, when I last saw you and asked you how you were, you just lifted your eyes and pointed upwards; the stroke had taken all your words and indecipherable whispers were all that were left.

Of all the men I have ever known you had the most beautiful voice – wild flowers and whisky, that's what it was. You also had one of the loudest voices, especially when something enraged you, which was usually the weather, the milk marketing board, sometimes Guy and, once in a while, me.

On the first occasion I stayed at New House Farm you asked me at supper what the weather would be doing in the morning. 'You're doing geography A level,' you said. 'You must be an expert in climatology by now.' It was a challenge as much as a game; I could see it in your eyes. I looked at the pressure charts in the newspaper and declared it would be a fine day. I didn't see you when I arrived in the milking sheds at four thirty the next morning; you were apparently brooding in the dairy. It was pouring with rain and I had quite forgotten our conversation of the night before. When you did show yourself your face had thunder in it, your eyes were loaded: 'I thought you said it was fucking well going to be sunny.'

You were clearly not that impressed either when I tipped up once at one in the morning, wearing nothing but black tie and a dress suit. The door to the house was locked so I broke a few bales and slept in the barn; I say 'slept' – it was February and there was frost on the ground. When I did make it to the milking sheds just after 5 a.m., I think, you were standing there, surrounded by steaming Jerseys. 'What time do you call this?' you fired at me.

'I've no idea,' I said, 'I couldn't get into the house and I haven't seen a clock. I did try and call to say I'd be in later than expected, but no one answered the phone . . .'

'No, you're quite right I don't answer the phone after nine o' clock at night – I'm a dairy farmer. Us dairy farmers, we have to get up at four, and so do the people who supposedly help them.' And then you handed me a yard broom and a pair of wellingtons.

Coming to visit your farm as a child was one of the greatest delights of my life. I'm so glad that my own children were able to see the place on a summer's day: to stand in the blocks of light cast across the floor by the glassless windows of the calf pens, amongst all that emptiness and vastness; to breathe the smell of water in the milking sheds; to listen to the corrugated roof, which holds every whisper and the arguing of sparrows which disappear into corners and fall out of nests.

Your house was a wonderland of jewels and gems, sparkling Victorian shoe buckles, porcelain figurines, silver boxes and carpets on the worn red-brick floors. And that window in the kitchen – the one above the table – that is my favourite window in the world, set deep and small into the thick stone. Then there were the oil paintings of your mother wearing pearls, I think, and your brother, who was killed running on to the beach on the morning of the D-Day landings. Your other paintings were more abstract – charcoal trees, a land covered in strange greens cows splashed onto board, a group of dancers and that painting of a boy by Augustus John.

In your small study next to the kitchen there were those pictures of faces on the walls and the china horses on the windowsill. In the bathroom at the top of steep stairs, you had arranged your hairbrushes on small chest beneath a mirror with flowers painted into it. Going to your house was like visiting another world – none of my friends' parents lived in anything like it. You created an *excelsis*, a *hosanna* to life, to colour, to form, to feeling. In all those rooms I was thrust inside the kaleidoscope; I became part of it.

I loved the way you talked to the cat, how you called her darling. She had been wild and there were all those endless feral kittens running around like mice in the barns, unbrushed and spitting. Guy's dog had most of them. Anyway, the cat too fell under your spell, like everyone who came to New House Farm. You created beauty, not to impress or because there was any financial gain in it for you. There was nothing ostentatious about your home – you

were a tenant farmer, you didn't own a brick to your name
– no, it was just because you enjoyed it. For you, beauty was
a creative act. It wasn't about ownership; it was about
enjoyment.

Your garden was the same. I'm sure some people might
have called it a mess: you just bought the odd plant and let
things happen around them. You were the only man I knew
as a child who loved roses.

I guess I realised you were gay in my teens. Daphne
would always deny it, but I think she was in love with you
once. All the women loved you, they adored you, but
you never let them close. They heard the voice, saw the
dancing eyes and I would imagine ten seconds later they
were dreaming . . .

And I loved you too. I loved you from the first moment
I met you limping around your kitchen. I must have been
about ten years old at the time. 'Do you know what is the
most up-to-date appliance I have in this kitchen?' you
asked. And you took S and me by the hand and led us to a
can-opener mounted on the wall. 'It's this. They're marvellous things, so modern,' and you proceeded to open cans of
Coca-Cola for us.

And you understood things; you understood how fascinating birds' eggs were – maybe because you recognised what jewels were. When I came back inside, having relieved a blackbird of one of her eggs, you held it in the palm of your hand and told me how beautiful it was. And I knew that you really *knew* how beautiful it was to me. No one else did – they couldn't feel it – but I knew you could. You knew how really beautiful it was.

You also knew pain. You lived with pain every day after driving over that landmine in Normandy, when it blew up your Jeep, blew off half of your back. Daphne told me the story of how the doctors said you would never walk again, how your mother pushed you around in a pram for two years afterwards, and how it was nothing other than your sheer bloody-mindedness that got you walking again. I knew you didn't like to discuss it. You would only let Guy or Sarah dress the wound, and the skin would constantly crack and bleed. It became more painful as you got older, the nerve endings turning to knives.

I suppose I let you be my father and that much of me now comes from you. Like your way of seeing children as eternally fascinating; I remember how you would lean slightly forward and look straight into my eyes without blinking; you would be bursting with enthusiasm for whatever I carried in my mind or held in my hand. I do this too with children, because I remember how it made me feel so special, to be cherished in that way.

And you were always so open about your failings. Maybe it had something to do with being so badly wounded that you were able to be so beautifully flawed. There was the time when you came to one of Daphne's drinks parties and there was one of those lulls in the conversation – the angels were flying over – and suddenly a voice came from a corner of the room: 'Christ, I'm pissed.' Then you hobbled outside and fell over in the roses. I think you drove home that night as well. Some years later, when you were eventually prosecuted for being over the limit, you just shrugged your shoulders. We all drove you around to your favourite antique shops, to the farm suppliers and into the village. I remember you appeared very relaxed about the fact that I didn't have a licence at the time either.

Much like David Bartleet, you were a very different type of man. Sometimes the farm was 'up' and we ate beef. Sometimes it was down, and you sold your pictures and waited for the good times again. I also saw how much you cared for your Jerseys; how you wouldn't let the old ones be put down because they no longer produced milk, how you gave them a field of their own and let them live out their lives. You always had to go inside when the hunt arrived to pick up the male calves – you hated the thought of what would happen to them, but there was nothing else you could do.

Thank you for letting me sleep in the oast house in that room upstairs at the back; I loved being there. I know I told you it was because I wanted to write – well, it wasn't that really. It was somewhere to go with girlfriends, though none of them liked it, with the mice running round underneath, the spiders hiding in the dust and the sill under the window covered in butterflies' wings.

You were always very unjudgemental about relationships. I wanted you to meet the girlfriends I had, but I know the only one you really took to was Jacs. And she adored you, as the children did later. I loved your routine whenever you met Charlotte or Claire – how you would start taking the mickey out of me, how you would set me up on a point of difference you knew we had, such as the environment.

You would cunningly steer my girlfriend round to your way of thinking and then at the critical moment turn to her and say, 'Are you sure you can't do better than this?' Then, gesturing in my direction, maintaining eye contact with her you would raise your eyebrows and say, 'Him, I mean.'

Sometimes you were distant and sometimes you were cruel to Sarah, but you were the most charming man I have ever met. I loved the way we could talk about pasture and films, God and woodpeckers, and all the names you gave your cows – Clarissa, Melody, Birthday, Cecilia; I remember how the names were written in chalk above their stalls.

Thank you for all that you gave me. I will try not to waste a second of it.

Peter

Dear Daphne,

Thank you for lunch the Sunday before I left to come here. It seems very far away now. And thank you for collecting me from the adoption agency forty-nine years ago.

I could have been placed with anyone. Whoever else it had been, my life would surely have been very different. Your life and my life would both have been very different if biology had dealt you another hand.

I think I remember you telling me that you had been engaged twice before you married Alan. You have never discussed with me who the other young men were, but you did tell me once you were a debutante. I can imagine you all in white at a party. And you have often told me how shy you were when you were young. Was it Alan's death that brought about a change? It must have been about six weeks after he had died that I went into your bedroom – it always smelt so lovely, of cream, with all those tiny bottles on your glass-topped dressing table – and you were getting ready to go to a party. You were dressed up in what appeared to be no more than a ballerina's tutu and a white shirt, and I think you were wearing suspenders. You told me it was a fancy dress party and that you were going as a cigarette girl. I knew then that you felt you had to change, that you were practically shaking off all the convention that goes with being 'a doctor's wife'. Even at the age of five, I could see that you weren't a doctor's wife any more.

Thank you for taking me to the heronry in Sussex when you weren't really interested in birds or butterflies. And thank you for coming with me when I waded out into the pond to help myself to a moorhen's egg. I never understood why you hated swimming but loved the sun.

I felt how hard life was after Alan died. The consequences of his death were bewildering and painful; he was no longer there and it was as if the real world had come barging into our lives. I was suddenly aware of money, which had become this heavy weight. I remember standing in front of the cold meats counter in the international stores in Edenbridge and you asked what I would like for lunch. I pointed to some beef and you had to tell me it was too expensive. I felt dreadful for having made you say that and insensitive that I hadn't even considered the cost.

When Alan died, you had to go work. First you had a job in the antique shop and then you started commuting up to London every day to be a personal assistant in a firm of solicitors in Jermyn Street. Whenever I went there it looked so dreary – it was like going into a fridge where everything was past its sell-by date.

I'm sorry I decided one afternoon that public school wasn't for me, but I think you always suspected it wasn't. I know you always wanted the best for S and me, but I'm afraid trying to herd me into the claws of the establishment was never going to work for either of us. The way I was treated by several of your male friends convinced me that those sorts of establishment men cared little for anything other than themselves: if the chips were down they would have no qualms about being unscrupulously ruthless. (And really – all that disapproval about the length of my hair or the fact that my jeans were torn . . .)

I know you were trying to protect me. You knew far

better than I did then how the world works – the importance of connections and reputations, and how if you acquired both the money would follow. But those men paid for power with their souls and then they crushed their souls simply to have more of it. Their trade was control – they had to control, they still do – but such control is an illusion albeit a very powerful one. In their eyes, I was a problem and so they treated me like one. But I am so sorry that I caused you pain. You were always so brilliant, so completely fair, and however badly I behaved I had a feeling you always forgave me. I hoped you could see that, despite appearances, I had no intention of wasting my life.

Thank you for letting me sleep with my girlfriends when most of my other friends were holed up in some car in the woods or dashing upstairs together whilst their parents walked the dog. As you said, you felt it was hypocritical to do otherwise. I agree it's far better to be honest and open about teenage sexuality. And although I know you still have your doubts, I think you were right to take the same line as far as hash was concerned. And I know your attitude must have taken a lot of courage, but courage is something you've always had in spades. What it meant in practice was that I didn't have to get stoned in darkness; and because I didn't have to hide the fact that I was smoking cannabis it was much easier to understand what a soul-destroying thing it is to do – to volunteer yourself for oblivion.

Despite appearances I have always tried to please you. I've been aware that I have a duty to give you happiness and, because I am so proud of you, I've wanted to behave in a fashion that makes you proud of me. Your approval and your blessing have always meant so much to me and I seek them still. Perhaps we are forever a child until our parents die and I reckon there's a good twenty years left in you yet. So doubtless we will continue our sparring for a long time to come. You will continue to ask me whether I 'have heard from the Bishop' and I will continue to tell you I have no need of hearing from the Bishop.

I admire your energy tremendously. You have always driven your car as if you're late which means that, as children, we always arrived early wherever we were going. I was usually the first to arrive at parties, often almost in time to see the magician putting his white rabbit up his sleeve and usually in time to find a row of empty tables with no sweets or biscuits set out on them yet – only some ruddy-faced grandfather blowing up balloons in the corner. Do you have a fear of being late or is it that you just want the best seat? S and I often speak about whether it's actually safe for you to belt around the countryside in the way that you do, but then I can't think of another woman in her late seventies who has such a rich and varied social life.

Your friends have really stood by you, despite the fact that every third glass of wine you drink has a mad dog in it who just wants to bark and have an argument, usually about politics; but that's fine. I know that now. Despite the mad dog in the third glass, you have always been incredibly generous – forever bringing presents and flowers, bursting through the door like a Russian aristocrat in a hurry – even when I knew you couldn't afford to be, and that you still can't. You are a truly elegant woman and I think it's great that you still find twenty-two-year-old Greek waiters dishy.

You are not so good with babies though; then you become nervous and clumsy. I know that your parents used to have you dressed up and presented to them whilst they sat there, sipping gin and tonics in India or Shanghai. As a child you spent more time with nannies than you did with them. I admire you for letting that crazy Rothmans-smoking mother of yours move in with us. She was always great at Christmas, plying me with Babycham. I remember once, when I must have been about twelve, she attacked all the wrapping paper on Christmas Day and took it outside to burn it, but set fire to several of our presents at the same time. To make up for it later in the evening, when we were sat watching television, this hand holding a packet of cigarettes appeared in front of me: 'Oh for goodness' sake take one – they go so well with Babycham.'

I really loved her – loved her as a child loves. And I really love you. I should have told you that many years ago.

Please, if you ever get to the point when you just want to sit around drinking Babycham and reading, when you have outlived all your friends and there is no one left to visit, S and I have agreed that you should know you can come and live with either of us.

Peter

Dear God,

Thank you for this day, for all days, for this moment.

Do we perceive time because our life here on this beautiful planet is limited, our flesh destined to become something else? The chameleon eats the flies and when she dies the flies eat the chameleon – there's this constant exchange of form, of grass becoming soil, soil becoming grass, grass becoming bread, bread becoming flesh, flesh becoming death, death becoming space, space becoming life. Does this process embody time? And is it linear or circular or formless? Today, it feels circular in the sense that it has no destination: it just is. Or, as you apparently said: 'I am.'

Why is it that children can perceive you and your closeness more clearly than adults? Is it because when we are children, our experience of reality has not hardened yet – in the sense that reality seems new and more permeable? And is it that, when we are young, we don't believe that we're right? We haven't attached ourselves to principles and roots, to old things, to notions of 'belonging' and ideas in a thousand shapes and forms, because everything appears new to us, nothing is old.

Maybe at that stage there is more osmosis; we have not imposed ourselves on reality. The piano plays and we become the notes, which in turn become a butterfly. We lie down behind the sofa and smell the dust. (Adults don't lie down behind sofas or hide in the washing; adults never get such a good look at shoes.) Too soon we go to school and there is almost a line of adults queuing up to inform us that one thing is older than another; that one idea, one place, one reality is holier than another – by which they invariably mean that you made it, you thought it. But as Einstein said, the fish will be the last to discover water.

I must have been about seven years old. It was spring and there was this hedge beneath a neglected apple tree. The tree wasn't in leaf but I could see the colour of the blossom through the bud casings. I was looking for nests. There was one in the hedge which belonged to a hedge sparrow. They are such demure little birds – I've never seen one fighting or squabbling, remonstrating like the sparkling starlings or the feisty house sparrows, never seen them drawing blood from their neighbours like robins do. As you know, for their nests they weave grass and hair precisely into a small deep bowl, which they line with moss to the point where it shines. And there they were – four varnished blue eggs sitting in this deep smooth green. This creation didn't feel like an act of power or strength or majesty; it was an expression of intimacy. It was delicate, silent like your gaze. We were both in a state of wonder and whilst I was alone, I realised I wasn't alone – that you were there in that state of wonder, you were present.

There is an open door from the room of wonder to the room of praise, where creation continually celebrates its being. All I was doing that spring day was joining in, giving myself a voice with which to sing. It was a celebration: you in celebration of us; us in celebration of you; you in celebration of you and us in celebration of us. It was continuous and in all things. The way autumn celebrates death, winter celebrates sleep, spring celebrates rapture and summer glory. How silence celebrates sound and sound celebrates silence.

I had no idea how long I let you hold me for that day, how long we had been together. I learned as I grew older that this was your love: you loving me and me loving you. We were in a state of love, and it was mutual and unconditional and really so simple. I gave it freely, you gave it freely until there was no you, there was no me – there were no rooms.

But when I went to school all this changed. And I was put under huge pressure to change with it. There were these adults who kept telling me how big you were, how great you were, how clever you were and how important you were. They expected me to tell you this, to sing to you, and they separated you from me. They taught me loneliness and said that if I misbehaved I would be punished by you. Then they told me I'd been born in sin and I was to ask you to forgive me because of this sin that someone called Adam had committed.

More importantly they claimed they knew you much better than I did – they knew all about you. But they didn't seem to know you at all. When they wanted me to stand there and praise you, I told them that I didn't feel it: there was no wonder. They didn't seem to me to know how to wonder; perhaps they weren't interested in wonder. They just wanted me to believe, to believe in you, and if I didn't believe, you would punish me. More often than not this was an excuse for them to punish me.

They made you so big, so strong, so terrifyingly powerful, that I was to get down on my knees in your presence. If I made myself small enough, only then would I be able to see how big you really were and how lost I really was.

They almost succeeded, as Jim Morrison has said, in 'tying you with fences'. On the other side of their fences was indeed the land of the lost and if I went there I would become foul and stained and fond of flesh – especially my own. I was to be forgiven when I came back again to the light side of the fence, but only on the condition that I told you where I had been and more importantly what I had been doing. But on the many occasions I have visited that dark and fascinating land, in all those dark rooms of forgetting, you are there waiting. And you bring me back through the couple walking arm in arm, the man in the café listening, the underside of leaves, just one glimpse of wonder – that's all it takes to find love again. In some of those rooms, the very worst of those rooms, there appears to be a total absence of love. Then it can be very hard to feel you.

Love speaks the language of wonder. I am amazed at how beautiful, how selfless, how brave, how intricate, how honest, how fragile it is. Your love has to express itself, *has to*, yearns to; it is earthed in yearning. As I get older it seems clearer to me that we don't describe you adequately – that we do not express your power in its true selflessness, intricacy, honesty, fragility. No, we seem to be obsessed with majesty and with an image of you as the founder of the universe, the mover of moons, the one who can change the colour of the skies. We gave you power over us and soon afterwards you became a dictator in our minds, issuing decrees about what to wear, what to eat, who to sleep with, when to stand, when to sit, when to pray, when to dance. And because we imagined your power was expressed in this way, we have assumed that imposition is the right of the powerful. We have made ourselves kings in this image. We looked to our distorted image of you for our blueprint of power, which we then made manifest. And it has set solid in each one of us.

When you gave us dominion over the fish of the sea, the birds of the air, the animals of the forest and the field, we exercised this great gift as domination. The hedge sparrows, the chameleons and the starlings are terrified of us. It is this model of power that is in the process of condemning much of the natural world, your gift to me, into oblivion or permanent imprisonment. The only way to stop this, I have decided, is to accept it personally: your gift of dominion was given to each one of us individually, not to the government or to farmers or to national park managers, or to the Church. No, it was given to me. It was given to us.

At least up here in this desert cave, which feels like the moon, I can pretend I am not part of that any more. Here, it is just you and me, and our brothers and sisters the flies. Maybe that is how it always is. I need to learn that I don't need to be strong any more and that all these tools I have acquired to make me strong are no more than embodiments of my fear, perversions of my fragility. I am so wonderfully fragile but so very afraid of that. I am learning here that I need to be weak, beautifully weak, so weak that – as the sadhus say in India – I dissolve.

All my love as ever,

Peter

Dear Jim,

Did you want to die in Paris? There was a time when I was younger when I wanted to visit your grave there, but I'm glad I didn't. They say it's covered in graffiti with bits of the stone chiselled off. It's become a shrine, you're venerated now – a poet, a prophet, not quite a saint; you would never have wanted to be a saint.

I can't remember the first time I heard 'Riders on the Storm'. It might have been at Steve's farm up in his attic bedroom. I have no recollection of buying *L.A. Woman*, though I remember selling my copy in Caterpillar Records in Notting Hill – I needed the money to buy hash. I wish I'd kept it: you sounded so great on vinyl. I played and played that LP until the notes and the words became part of the soil in my soul.

Recently I bought a DVD, with you in black and white

on the cover, looking like King David. You wrote like him, painting the present into the eternal. He too, like you, expressed the other, the unseen, the liminal. Why were you so keen to acknowledge it, this other world that I felt and you saw? You sang it; you wrapped it in words. Your songs were filled with an acceptance of being separate. They came from a place apart, from a place beyond almost marooned from reality: 'I am a passenger, I ride and I ride' '. . . into this house we're born, into this world we're thrown . . . riders on the storm.' You expressed the sense – the suspicion – that as human beings we are just visiting this planet and that we are really a very long way from home, exiled here. Normality – you know: cars and meals, bathrooms and shoes – all this is at best just dull, no more than functional, to the point where either through necessity or choice we as human beings find ourselves experiencing life as something functional rather that something spiritual.

It is said that childhood is the bank upon which all writers draw. I can only say that as a child I was aware of this 'other' that came to be called God, or at least I was encouraged to call it God. To me, it was the creator of birds' eggs, the light on the underside of leaves and the marvellous wings of butterflies. Somehow, whilst I could see all this and feel its wonder, I was separate from it; I could be held by it but I wasn't it – the umbilical cord had been cut. I remember how you sang from the perspective of being in a strange land, amazed at its beauty on one hand and on the other saddened by the way human beings like us relate to the experience of being alive – how we are prone to cheapen it, to buy it and sell it and languish rather than live.

You found solace in women; I'm not sure they ever found solace in you. I got the impression you enjoyed their attention and their bodies, their breath on your skin, but really it was never going to last because you were in love with Nature, with her detail and her distance. You knew that the only thing of permanence is the fact that everything is forever changing, and when you cried out 'what have they done to the earth . . . tied her with fences and dragged her down', you were railing against the fact that our treatment of this beautiful planet is far from an act of celebration. You saw all this.

Was it pain that made you drink? A critic once said of you that he never knew if he was going to meet the erudite poet or the barroom drunk. I have a feeling you used to drink until your lights went out – until all you could feel was nothing. No detail, no distance, no breath. And then of course there were the drugs. You could say you were following in Aldous Huxley's footsteps, experimenting with perception, or it might be better to say testing reality.

You see, reality is so flimsy, isn't it? It's no more than a convenience. There are so many different realities happening in so many different rooms. The reality of flies, the reality of chameleons, the reality of horses, the reality of the child in a room in an Egyptian village, the reality of the woman walking down Sloane Street and, oh yes, the reality of the Christian, the Jew, the Hindu, the Muslim.

The man who comes up to you on the street corner and tells you God is love; the young woman who hands you a leaflet extolling the virtues of vegetarianism – all this you knew is just a matter of perspective. I can attach myself to whatever reality I choose and if it makes me feel better – great, but don't go trying to impose your reality on me, I will not let you take away my freedom in that manner, I will not be controlled by your version of reality. Yes, you're right: there are so many from which to choose, aren't there? So many different versions to experiment with that to conform to one at the price of deriding the others is to diminish the experience of being human. Ultimately we diminish ourselves.

So what you offered me was freedom to test reality; you encouraged me to do so and you confirmed that there is life in so many different forms, in so many different rooms.

I wonder if you hadn't drunk yourself to death that night in Paris whether you would have stopped shouting at God for abandoning you into this lonely place. Would you have seen beyond the moribund plaster cast of divinity dressed up as sanctity by most churches, temples and mosques? Would you have found God like another singer called Mike Scott said – 'where he always was' – or would you have held fast to Job and continued throwing your stones? I throw stones too.

There were two men who gave me a vision of what life could be – of the huge potential that it holds, that we hold. One expressed it quietly and the other colourfully, but you sang it out for the world to hear. And your voice travelled into the attic of a farmhouse in England: it was so exciting, so full of promises. It offered a ticket into other worlds, not that I don't like this one – I do – but because you made being here bigger. You showed me that there was more to this life than owning, controlling and proving; that there was an awful lot of experimenting and experiencing to be done.

Thank you,

Peter

Dear Satan,

I've often thought about what fuels your tenacity, your stubborn insistence. You will never give up; you will continue this fight because you are so utterly relentless. But what fuels your hatred? I can understand that you should desire my hatred of everything and most of all myself. That is what you need me to feel – to feel the full force of hatred, the jagged spark that lights the flames – but what made you hate to start with? What made you this teacher of hatred?

You must be delighted with our portrait of hell and how comical it has become: shrivelled little men with misshapen eyes and yellow tongues rounding up all your human slaves with children's swords and beefeaters' axes. And are you pleased with your own image as well? A masterful creation, I might add – that red-faced, red-tailed man with horns carrying a trident. You seem to laugh a lot as well; it's a deep laugh but it's the last laugh.

And there you are, starring in *Tom and Jerry* and a thousand advertisements to quit smoking. You look like a figure of fun so we don't have to take you seriously. We certainly don't have to be afraid of you, which is, of course, the great deception. No, you taught us long ago to be afraid of you: when we were at the bottom of the stairs and it was dark; when we dreamt of dogs who could speak and who told us how good our flesh tasted. You taught us to fear through those who discovered fear is an effective means of control. You control through fear; your food is fear. Because once we fear – once we have ingested even the tiniest drop of terror – then we have opened an account with you. And then you will do anything, you will use anything, to teach us that there is so much to be afraid of. At first fear is still a choice – until we forget we choose to be afraid. Then we are close to oblivion.

Loss is inevitable, so why do I fear it? To make mistakes is human so why do I hide them? One bed is enough – why should I need more? And I think back to all those times when I worried that one pair of trousers might be better than another; that if my lucky bean were to crack I would surely die; that the single magpie was me; that the quiet of the night was you. The only way round you and beyond you, beyond these worries – these fears, all fears – were the anaesthetics of beer, beef and hash; of another bed and of another human being like me. Another person who had been taught to worry that they were not beautiful enough to be loved, so they sought comfort in that pit of loneliness; but still they could not find love and so they felt themselves more unloved and were less and less able to love themselves. They say it's a slow road to oblivion but there are faster ones, aren't there? The more hate we ingest, the more fuel we have to kill. But it's not the death of the flesh you are really concerned with – it's the death of the soul that you want, isn't it? You want to take away God's love from the object of God's love, which is creation itself. It takes a much longer game-plan to obliterate that, to achieve your victory of complete oblivion.

To start with, you need us to believe that creation itself is primarily dangerous: it is a danger to us so we need to control it and to impose our will on it using the most violent means at our disposal. The ground that cannot give us food you call wasteland, barren, waste ground. And then, because we are afraid that it might not rain or we are afraid that it might freeze, you say to each one of us that creation itself is ours. 'Take it all,' you said. 'Just in case. Oh yes, you can have it all – you are kings. You can have the sea; you can have the hills; you can have the hens; you can have the gold; you can have the cows and the whales; and you can have all of those delicate hedge sparrow's eggs, all of them. Take all of them.'

But none of these things was ever yours to give. Once you had stolen them and given them to us, we became afraid of losing them so we began to own them. I noticed you tried that with Jesus. You tried to give him all these things, but he knew they were not yours to give and he understood that the price for agreeing to accept them would be dreadful for human beings, who would be enslaved by you as a result. It wasn't a decision he took for himself; he took it for me.

The older I become the more I see you as a choice. At the end we leave behind us the sum of our choices. At this particular moment I am all the choices I have ever made. Some of them were very ugly and I have learned that unless I can face them full on, understand the root of them, they will continue to be a part of me. Jesus says 'know yourself' and it is really only by knowing the reality of their existence that I can begin to deal with my choices. The small print at the base of advertisements is always much more revealing than the ads themselves.

As you know, it is much easier not to take responsibility for anything and I worry that we have made you so terrible by giving you responsibility for the terrible things and the ugliness we dare not own up to. And I often wonder whether Jesus was able to love you.

I don't know whether we will ever update our vision of hell. I'm not sure hell really exists. I think loneliness exists, bleakness exists, futility exists, but hell – no, I'm not inclined to fear your hell. But I am more and more concerned about those who seem so keen to make me afraid of it. No, hell is much quieter than they are, isn't it?

All my love,

Peter

Dear Jesus,

I've been dreading writing this letter. There are a few people who have a knack of making me feel bad about myself – like I just don't quite come up to the mark – and I suspect they use their disapproval as a form of control. Right now up here on the moon, with nothing but desert, that's how I feel about you. Don't get me wrong – I admire you tremendously, but you are distant and serious. I look at you and think of how many eggs I have broken.

Maybe it's down to where I put myself in relation to you. When I was training to become a priest I remember the principal of the theological college saying that we meet you on Good Friday, when we stand before the foot of the cross. And that's about as close as I have ever been. Most of the time I am in the crowd watching you, listening; I am listening intently.

To be honest, I find your Father much easier to be with. He seems less abrasive and much more relaxed. He does lead me beside still waters. But with you there are few points of stillness; you seem caught up in this narrative that you are writing and directing, and you are so busy, so full of words. I accept that this distance is something I have created and whilst I would love to be one of your disciples I don't feel good enough – or maybe I am just not prepared to give up everything, to give up all of me and give it to you, to God, which is what you ask for.

I think theology has a great deal to do with it. As I get older I find what you said about this experience – about living and about being human – more and more radical, more and more exciting; but I am teaching myself to hear what you say from outside the boundaries of Christianity. I imagine that there is no such thing as Christianity and all I am doing is hearing your words, hearing them before you died – before you came back as the Son of God, a king; before there were any churches; before there was Easter, Christmas, the Father, the Son and the Holy Spirit; before all that was dreamt. And, beyond all that noise, what you have to say about the personality of God and the depth of human being is increasingly utterly compelling to me.

Statements such as 'knock and the door shall be opened' have become Christian teachings, but they were not originally meant as such. No, surely you spoke these words to express how you felt, to try to explain how close we are to the divine and how close we are to being divine. The more we rely on knowledge, on 'knowing', the further we are marooned from feeling and then we become heavy: this forgetting of feeling is heavy, an eternal tiredness.

You were so awake – you felt everything, didn't you? You could feel others when they were afraid; you could feel their loss, their pain. You could feel how beautiful the lilies were, couldn't you? And you could feel how empty the Church had become, how utterly consumed by the seduction of the empirical, how we had abandoned our sensual nature. God, you were so sensual. It was Eckhart Tolle who showed me how to feel your words: he poured water over them and they opened like lilies. They became alive, yet to get to those words I have had to go through them.

I am not sure any more whether we have any right to trade under your name. Also, I have to say that as a Church of England vicar I am increasingly uneasy about what has happened to all your words. And I am even more uneasy about what has happened to you. You have been placed above us, not beside us. Your followers have become part of the very power structures you came up against. It wasn't the political establishment you angered; it was the religious establishment who had fallen in with the politicians, who had really become politicians – they had looked to the system to protect them rather than God. Quite rightly, you pointed that out; you made them aware that this kind of compromise was wretched and you showed them that believing in love is a very dangerous thing to do. Love is always at odds with order and always threatens the construct of order. So to maintain the construct they killed you.

I find nothing extravagant in your return. I am interested in what form you took – whether it was your body or your soul. To me, death is a doorway that we all pass through to return home; so to arrive here, all you did was blur the edges. Did you travel between the two states of life and afterlife? Yet again, this is where theology is simply insufficient. Theology states that your life was preordained by God: that in dying you were fulfilling God's plan and that you were preordained to die at the hands of human beings – which rather worryingly means they must have been preordained to murder you.

In the current climate I find it increasingly unpalatable to believe that your death was necessary to prove your father's love and that your death proved your love for us and for your father. Cannot life become a metaphor for love? Life as love: can that not be as potent as death as love?

I think my favourite passage in the New Testament is about the storm on the Sea of Galilee. You were asleep, which means you were tired – and I am so glad you were tired. I can understand that. I was in India a couple of months ago, living with sadhus and their guru, and that's how it was, wasn't it? – Like them, you and your disciples were itinerant and you were revered as a teacher, as a holy man. Really you were a traveller; as you said: 'Foxes have holes but the son of man has nowhere to lay his head.'

The more I hear about your life, the more it seems that everything started to unravel when Mary Magdalene came on the scene. I don't see that necessarily as a bad thing; your relationship with her is self-consciously ambiguous at best. She clearly loved you, loved you completely, but I feel – well, I know – that the amount of time and attention you gave Mary caused huge tensions within your group of male disciples. (Why did you choose only men?) I don't think they would have said what they are supposed to have said unless they felt that the love you had for her was pulling you away from them. Did it? Or was it just part of the mix?

Is human love the same as divine love? When we love are we experiencing divinity? Are we experiencing eternity? Is love the expression of our beautiful self? Do we meet with the divine in this state? Some of your followers today claim to know your answers to these questions, but I don't have any answers – I only have questions and the older I get the more questions I have, and the more I see you as a guide rather than a god.

I have a feeling that how we find you, or indeed how you find us, is not really as important as how we *behave* having found you. Not how we behave outwardly, but how we behave inwardly. And it's about whether we are able to stick to truth, to our truth, or whether we pick it up and put it down whenever it suits us. I am so very guilty of that.

You speak to the inner being that exists in all of us – the 'ground of being' as one writer has put it. Of course you are there on the inside; there isn't a storm, a desert, a moon – there is nothing to perceive outwardly, is there? Consciousness is internal. I have only met one human being who shattered the door between the inner person and the outer person, and who engaged my inner being; and it was as if I had always known her. She made me aware of love, the well of love that lies inside all of us. You do the same. Whilst I need words to explain, I don't need words to experience it. Something happens to us and we find ourselves beyond ourselves.

I read in Mark that you went off into the wilderness, into the wild places, to pray early, before everyone else was up. It was to find yourself in God, wasn't it? – to experience the limitlessness of physical being, to enter knowing without learning and love without fear. Somehow all that has become not that, if you know what I mean. When faith solidifies it becomes religion and the most solid things we have are your words. We have made towers out of your words, buttresses and spires.

And up here on the moon, I can hear the rocks expanding and contracting; I can hear a thousand flies speaking all at once. The stones have taught me how one-dimensional words are: how words convey meaning but are not meaning in themselves; they are wineskins not the wine. Words can turn diamonds into glass, wine into water, girls into goats, Christians into infidels and sadly some young Muslims into bombs. Words can usually do anything the writer or the speaker wants them to do. Is this what you were trying to save us from – our need of words, our reliance on just words? Because you knew how solid they can become and how that solid state, or rather our belief in it, denies the truth that everything is fluid. And nothing in this universe is stationary, is it?

We are not stationary, are we? The sky, the grass, trees, living, dying, loving, hating – there is constant movement and there is no beauty without it. You were fluid, weren't you, and that's why you could feel and flow between life and death; why of course you saw no necessity to own anything. The illusion of possession, of ownership, is so very powerful that when we attach ourselves to possessions we become less fluid and thereby less capable of feeling. I am concerned about those who attach themselves to you.

Thank you for your teaching: I have a lot to learn, even more to forget.

All my love,

Peter

Dear Al,

To be honest, I have no idea how it happened – where or how we just 'got' each other. I know I must have met you when I was about fourteen years old or so. I remember meeting your brother Mike: we were playing tennis, or rather he was playing tennis and I was just trying to hit the ball back.

And I remember that room at the end of your house which led on to the garden, where there was the hi-fi and we all signed the door. There were posters of Bowie, that self-portrait you did in oils and the paintings that marked the beginnings of Mike's journey into art. I loved all of them, especially your portrait.

Your house was quite dark and it felt like a hard place to heat. In the hallway, hanging high on the walls above barometers, there were all those stuffed impala heads that your parents had brought back from Africa. And the room with the piano in it was always full of boxes; the curtains seemed to be permanently closed.

The garden was truly wonderful – full of rooms, dells and shade where violets grew in between the stones. I loved the view of the field at the back of your house, where a solitary oak tree stood in the middle, taking the rain and hiding the owls.

You know, I have no sense of your moving there: it just seemed like you had always been there. And I don't think we have ever really talked about your childhood in Africa. All you will say about it is that Mike didn't speak for the first four years of his life, but I have always wanted to ask you what you saw there – what you brought back from there – because so much of your house felt as if something had been left behind in Africa.

And there is something in the photographs you now take and in Mike's paintings – his charcoal rhinos and oils of goalposts – as well as your own landscapes. They all have a light in them that I've only ever seen in Africa, when Jacs and I went to Kenya.

For some reason we thought it would be a good idea to

buy a mobile discotheque – and it was, it was a great idea – although to start with we had no idea what we were doing. I think we did it because for both of us music illuminated the world we saw, which, as you know, is always the world we happen to believe we see. There is essentially nothing beautiful that exists. It is when we see something as beautiful that it becomes beautiful and our own beauty is reflected in it. The same is surely true of music. There is something fabulous about being able to take part in something new. In the same way as beauty happens, an exchange takes place with music.

And what a ride it was – to have ingested all those Led Zeppelin albums and *Aladdin Sane*; God, all the energy of the Clash and the Pistols – to have been on all those waves. I don't miss them; I love them for what they were.

'The Mean Machine' was a dreadful name and I'm amazed anyone booked us. But they did – all those village halls and the Red Barn. And then there was that wedding, where Charlie drank an entire bottle of vodka, helped himself to a plateful of coronation chicken, ate too many gherkins and several slices of pâté, then wobbled to the front of the stage and threw up all over the wedding cake –

and into most of the champagne glasses. No, we didn't get paid for that one.

I remember once when we hired the Red Barn (well, I say 'we': you put the deposit down). I was at the front taking the tickets and you were inside on the decks, when Tom told me that a greaser had been down and informed him he was just off to rally the Hell's Angels, who would apparently be returning en masse with razor blades. Why I stood by the door for half an hour I don't know, but I do remember being frightened.

Anyway, after a while I assumed they weren't coming and went back inside. Then you said something and I said something. There was this tension between us. I took over from you and no one was dancing. You came up ten minutes later and said, 'Let it go.' You said everyone was picking up on the way we were feeling and that it was affecting everything. You were eighteen and you got that. I remember being amazed – not because you were right, but because no one had taught you that; it was something you just saw, felt and understood. And you really came to life in that moment. As Mike Scott later wrote, 'I saw the crescent, you saw the whole of the moon.'

Along with the discotheque came the farm labouring. I loved the time we spent on that farm in Dorset. That evening Jo, you and I headed off to Cerne Abbas. On the way back, one of us had the idea to swim in a lake we had passed on the way there. We pulled over by the side of the road and clambered through the hedge. Jo and I took off all our clothes and ran down to the water covered in the moon. And I remember diving in, swimming across and running up through the field on the other side, until I realised I had careered into a thistle patch. I was picking my way out when Jo appeared running up out of the dark. I can see her now – the grass up to her knees, her dark hair all over her breasts.

We swam back across the lake and, shivering, ambled up to where we had left you. You were just about out cold; it's the only time I've ever seen you drunk. You always had a stop button and I knew instinctively that I was safe with you when I was younger as mine didn't work that well. Invariably, because you knew when to stop, that meant you took responsibility – which was both a blessing and a curse, I think.

You went to art college in Manchester while I stayed in the sticks and latterly in London, hanging out in squats on Elsham Road with all those princes and thieves. I would

And you began to hold on to things. First it was the School for Economic Science, then homeopathy and your diet. (God, I've never seen anyone eat so many brown bread watercress sandwiches.) But none of it worked. You still continued to cough up blood and you slowly turned greyer and greyer. And then you got pleurisy and then you got it again.

It was do or die at the end, wasn't it? I really admired you for giving up all that you were holding on to. No, you were not well at all. The X-ray revealed a polyp on your lung. The surgeon went in through your back and removed it. When I visited you in hospital you said you just wanted to watch crap television and read rubbish books, and I knew then you were back: you had released yourself from your worst fears.

Your house in Brixton was great; so were the parties you and Mike had there. I remember coming to one of them and it taking two hours to get up the stairs – I wish we'd filmed them.

Do you think when we are eighty we will look back and realise how formative the years in our forties and fifties were? I'm not so sure. What perhaps neither of us realised when we were in our twenties – and thirties even – was that we were just deciding what to choose. Neither of us really understood the ideas we were gorging on, the abstracts we ingested, nor how all things combine all the time to continually create what is new.

We were not to know then that exchange is constant and that it is the flower that holds us as much as we hold the flower. That when you reach the place where you are not dominating the flower – when the ego has gone – you are no longer a superior being; rather, you are similar to, you are at one with, that which you see yourself in. That, perhaps, is the oneness of God.

I met Charlotte in the lift on her first day at work. It was like standing next to an angel. She was working downstairs while Jacs and I were upstairs. I picked up the phone and told you I had just met your wife. I had never used those words before and I've never used them since. You didn't seem too startled about the fact that you hadn't met her yet – you didn't believe me, did you, mate? God, I felt so pleased with myself at your wedding.

I have always admired the way you are as a husband; how when you had to go away you would hide Post-It notes around the house with messages on them, telling Charlotte how much you loved her. I love her, everyone loves her, Al; I know that is not easy sometimes.

Thank you for buying me all those meals in Poons when I never had any money. You have always been so generous and you have always told me the stuff I didn't want to hear, like that I needed to become more reliable, much more considerate, and to understand that there are always consequences. You opened so many worlds for me because I could share them with you, because I felt you knew them – you know them. Without your friendship I would never have understood how completely entwined all life is; that when we feed each other ideas and knowledge and intuition we are willing each other to fly.

Apart from the natural world, which you know I love, it is our friendship that has been the rock of my life. Really, so much has come from it – from the knowledge of its presence. Amazing how clear things become when you are without anything, really – when you let go like you have to up here on the moon. But you know that, don't you?

I still think you would make the most wonderful counsellor. You have been the most wonderful friend.

All my love,

Pete

Darling Jacs,

I never know what you are doing at two o'clock. Up here on the moon, I can imagine you in the mornings, grappling to get the children off to school; I can picture you when they return; and I can see you banging the pots on the cooker, turning everything up to full power just to cook spaghetti as quickly as possible. I never understood why, although you're such a good cook, you loathe cooking – I'm a crap cook but I love it.

You have the most beautiful eyes I have ever seen. They're what I've always imagined Helen of Troy's eyes must have been like. You were and you still are one of the most beautiful women I have ever met. I formed that opinion immediately, when I first saw you sitting in reception; before you told me I was hardly likely to get the job with holes in my jumper. I could accept that remark coming from someone in a Chanel two-piece. And I loved the way you breathed in before you announced the name of the advertising agency – you still do that now sometimes before you say something, especially when you have eye contact and when your first word is 'well' as in 'well, look at you' or 'well, that must mean he's insane'.

I loved the way you walked down Sloane Street like it belonged to you – it was your court. I loved your tenderness; you understood completely how to be tender and when our marriage was falling apart I just craved your tenderness. I was sitting around a fire with some Bedouin last week when the oldest of them asked me what had been the happiest day of my life. I told him it was our wedding day – it wasn't the happiest moment but it was the happiest day. I had never seen a pink wedding dress before and I haven't seen one since.

And do you remember how we made this vow, this pact that we weren't going to carry the past into the present? That the hurt we had both ingested, especially the dreadful things your father laid at your door, all of that was to be put behind us so our wonderful children would not have to endure it. It was such a noble concept but we know now that's all it ever could be, standing there believing that eggs don't crack. What it meant in practice was that neither of us dealt with what had hurt us. Whilst hope and love might have been able to outshine the demons, the demons were simply waiting for doubt to arrive and then back they crept through the cracks.

I loved our time in London, I loved being the two of us; I loved being with you – I still do. I loved just knowing you were in the next room and I loved waking up next to you.

Thank you for our children. I remember that day when we were both late for work and we were running up towards Hyde Park Corner to jump on a bus. You were out of breath and you said there was this taste of iron in your mouth. I knew then that you were pregnant, but I wanted you to tell me, to look me in the eyes, breathe in and say, 'Well, you'll never guess what the chemist gave me today and I don't even want you to think what I did with it, but I'm pregnant.' You're one of the bravest women I have met, physically brave to give birth to Eden and Harris at home despite the medical establishment not being so keen on the idea. I still have the picture of you lying naked on our bed with Eden inside you. It is beautiful.

When did we stop talking and why? I know how bad I am at discussing my feelings, how I prefer to use ink rather than sounds. But I can't remember a day when I ever thought 'this is going wrong' – it just went wrong and then, as far as you were concerned, it became wrong.

I think it's too easy to blame the Church of England, although really I had such a ridiculous notion of what being a parish priest was all about. I know, when I asked you to marry me, I said that was what I felt I would become – but neither of us were prepared for how destructive it would be for both of us. As your stepfather said, he could never see you as a 'vicar's wife'. No, you were never a vicar's wife – certainly not vicar's wife material – and I am so sorry you had to endure all that disapproval. Disapproval is a poison and both you and I have swallowed too much of it. I never disapproved of you and I never will.

There is a scene in a film called *Half a Sixpence* in which Tommy Steele and Julia Foster stand in front of an empty field, dreaming about the house he plans to build. Tommy Steele sees a large country house whilst Julia Foster imagines a small thatched cottage with a garden stuffed full of flowers. Unaware of each other's vision, they both turn to one other and agree how lovely it will be. I always dreamt of a country vicarage with a vegetable garden – a place where we could laugh, where it would be safe to cry, where we could encourage our children in the arts of love. It just goes to show how selfish I was, really: I didn't see what you saw and I should have asked you to describe it. And really I still don't know; I don't know what would be perfect for you.

Living in the vicarage in Haslingfield wasn't perfect for either of us, certainly not while there was a small group of people trying their utmost to get us to move out. I had to try to love them, and I couldn't tell you it was the hardest time in my life because I wanted to make it all OK. I wanted to walk through the door and leave all those difficulties behind, but I persevered. Maybe I shouldn't have done that – the cost, the emotional energy that it required from both of us, was too much. We both became ill and then one day you turned round and said you couldn't do it any more. 'You had to be you.' It was an incredibly brave thing to do and really saved both of us, I think.

But, still, I was never completely sure what you couldn't do any more. Was it the whole package or was it me? I think we had both understood by then that we needed entirely different things from life: things that neither of us could give the other and yet which in the end we needed more than we needed each other. I needed to grow vegetables and you needed to buy them washed and peeled. You needed purple and I needed green. What neither of us should have done was to punish the other for needing those things. We know that now. Similarly, our ideas about bringing up children could not have been more different, but we weren't to know that before we had them.

So now the children live in your house, the house you rent. God, I feel so terrible about that – how could I have been so stupid as to let the house we owned in London go simply because the Church didn't want me to go to theological college carrying a mortgage? And I am so sorry that our lives were awful financially from the moment I started training. Most of all I was pissed off I couldn't buy you stuff, like a car that worked, and even when we were both so tired, I couldn't take you away for a proper break, so we'd just stay at home.

We only ever got away once together during the entire time we had children. We went up to Blakeney, where we stayed in that hotel on the seafront, our room overlooking all that mist and marsh. And there was that meal in the evening and the conversation with that old soak at the bar, who said nothing good ever came out of Nuneaton. Then there was the one whole day we had on the beach at Burnham Overy Staithe, picking up different coloured stones and handfuls of razor shells.

I know work was an issue – how much time I wasn't at home and how much time my head wasn't there either. As well as meeting all the demands of being a vicar, I'd be churning out some wretched advertising campaign or glued into endless lines of ink which I had the ridiculous notion would make us some extra money.

Well, as you know, here I am now in this cave, looking out over the eastern desert. I bet you're thinking: 'You don't have to wash, shave, answer the phone – all you have to do is to lovey it up while millions of people watch you being the centre of attention. You love it, you know you do.' I admit that not shaving or washing is great – they're such a waste of time. And not answering the phone? – Yes I can live without that too. But I have never enjoyed being the centre of attention; that's always made me uncomfortable. What you see is the performer, the peacock with his feathers up, but he's just enjoying being the peacock: being the centre of attention has nothing to do with it.

What I always loved was your attention, how you would circle me like a swallow, taunting me that I could catch you but I'd have to be much cleverer than I was currently being. And how from the depths of those green eyes you would make fire and shake rooms and ideas and unmask all those pretenders. Having said that, you are an appalling judge of character – which is probably why you ended up with me.

I'm so sorry I missed Desmond's funeral. Jonnie told me you cried. I know you loved him and you knew I loved him too. Crying is wonderful . . . and I was thinking we could just meet – you and I – and take the winding lanes to Crowhurst, have a picnic in a field with wine, and then sit in the church and cry. Just hold each other. And then you could return to East Anglia and I to the South Coast, knowing everything was really all right between us; that we'd forgiven each other.

I remember one afternoon in Haslingfield when I was in the garden with that lovely priest, Rebecca's father, and we were working away, pulling on some ivy. We'd been silent for a couple of minutes when he stopped and looked into a window of the house. He must have seen you. He turned to me and said, 'You know, you married one hell of a woman.' And he was right.

All my love,

P.

Dear Gladys,

I'm dreaming of cow parsley, of Queen Anne's lace.

As you come off the A27 and drive into Firle, there is a small stretch of road no more than two hundred and fifty yards long. The trees have grown up on either side of it and in the winter, when they have lost their leaves, they take on the shape of huge perfect waves just on the point of breaking. And when the cow parsley comes into flower, it is like driving through the sea. I know you would understand that.

I learned so much about you in India. There, the Hindu faith revolves around gurus in ashrams. The gurus sometimes sit on slightly elevated platforms, where they can remain for hours, for days. Their followers gather around them. Some of them just want to be near the guru – simply to be in the guru's presence is enough; to absorb his or her stillness, tranquillity, peace. To be near you is the same: your presence is beautiful and everybody feels it. You radiate love and you are one of the few human beings I have met who can and does so; it seems natural to you, you have become love in so many ways. And it's not theoretical – it's not because you *believe* in love or in the purpose of love. There were times when you just *were* love and there was no need to believe in it any more.

That church was so forlorn, wasn't it? It was permeated with misery. It was as if God was ill, lying in a bed with dirty sheets, overcome with melancholy. Yet you were there. I slowly began to see you sitting by yourself in the pews, but you seemed in pain. In fact, everyone seemed in pain and exhausted by it. There was a tangible and utter absence of love and affection in that place – it was as if the whole space was full of brambles and everything had been overcome by a permanent dusk. It was like the castle in my story of the witch-catchers, who'd cut off children's fingers as a punishment for skipping and then use them to ward off evil spirits.

Their fingers were kept in a box and, day in, day out, they were counted over and over again by an elderly human being who had no idea why he was doing it, but he had reached the point where it was all he could do.

After a while I became very ill, you remember, when I had Bell's palsy. The right hand side of my face was paralysed, dead. The Archdeacon came round but only because Jacs had told him to. He stayed half an hour and the whole time he was like a child staring at a car crash. Then you started to come round. First of all you brought a cushion, then another one and another one, along with packets of biscuits and then flowers – beautiful, bright sweet peas, roses and lilies. You told me how much God loved us all, even the witch-catchers, and then you became an angel, really you did. You had probably always been one, sitting, praying, enduring; and you would speak about your family, how the grandchildren were doing at school, the tides of your children's relationships and I saw in you the first brimstone butterfly of spring. You were the Good Witch of the North who arrives at the end of *The Wizard of Oz* and says: 'I was always there, I was always with you, all you had to do was knock your heels together three times.'

When you prayed it was like a peace went through you and into everything around you; and if when you prayed you spoke it was as if you were praying *with* God rather than *to* God. I mean – how many things do we see in a day? Hundreds, thousands? And we pass through them all; we don't acknowledge them – we don't acknowledge the extraordinary miracle of this moment, not because we don't want to but because we think it isn't new. We think we know it so our heads take charge of our hearts and we don't feel it any more, don't feel our being any more.

It was such a gift being with you. I always felt better for being with you. You made everyone feel better about being themselves; you showed us the moment uncluttered by our desires and needs. You never expressed God as something separated from being. No, God was within us. There wasn't a good part or a bad part of creation; for you, decay was just as wondrous as birth. You bring out the beauty in everything – in everyone – and it was you who transformed the witch-catchers' castle in that church, it was your presence. You untied the brambles that had wrapped themselves around us and we weren't in pain any more.

I'm sure you must have been the most incredible sales assistant of all time. Someone would come into that clothes shop and try something on, and you'd tell them: 'You look lovely', and you'd really mean it and they would feel it. What you did was to make them feel lovely. And I love the way you'd laugh when people's hats fly off on bridges, and how you'd marvel at puppies and tell me the rain was warm, or that someone was a really good person and another was kind and another had a good heart. I think my favourite Christmas (apart from the one Jacs and I spent together in Bucks Mills just after we were married) was when you and Brian and some of your children and grand-children came to the vicarage. I don't recall anyone's face without a smile on it.

When you decided to become part of the Church, they gave you a blue stole at that service in Ely Cathedral. And your being made a Reader didn't make any difference at all, except sometimes the role made you tired.

Some days I dread you dying: the fact that you are here

now, but that one day you will become no more. As it says in the Psalms, '. . . and its place will know it no more'. I can see your sitting room, those charcoal drawings of audiences at the theatre, the way you have bottles of drink standing in a tray and your long coat hanging up by the door – you are always so elegant. What will happen to those things that once described something about you, like your recipe for courgette and spinach soup?

Men and women have such complicated relationships; there are so many different types of infinite variety. Our relationship isn't mother–son, although I'm of an age to be your son; nor are we lovers, and really 'friends' is too light a word. 'Intimates' perhaps? Ours isn't a relationship of minds or bodies; it is a relationship of souls. Is that eternal, do you think? Can I see you when I die – will you be there?

You know, I love Firle – just the colour of it, its shapes, its combinations of brick and flint, and how the house martins return every year to fill the street with their dancing; how the tarmac gives out just beyond my house, the shadows on the walls inside these rooms in the summer, the wild autumn storms. Do you think we spend our whole lives looking for places and people, searching for contact – looking to make real contact? There is this calling into communion with all life and when we find it – true communion – it wakes us like love, raises us from the dead.

I always miss you and I always love you,

Peter

Darling India, Jonnie, Harris and Eden,

I really hope you are well. I miss you all madly. By that I mean I miss you individually. The only friends I have here are flies and ants. There is a chameleon as well, but most of the time there is just silence – utter and complete silence. I thought I knew what silence was like but I didn't until I came here: I never knew it could be so noisy, so much happening inside it.

If you like tuna and sardines the food is fantastic; if you don't, it's awful because that's the only food there is here. Really, if you try to imagine Santa's grotto that's what this cave's like. It's a very, very small space full, it seems, of a lot of things – mostly pictures of Jesus – and at night there is a glow-in-the-dark Virgin Mary. Actually, it's a bit like living in the loft. There is no electricity, there are lots of boxes, you can't stand up, it's very dusty and it is so *so* hot. Imagine what it's like when Mummy turns the central heating up full and complains in June that 'It's so bloody cold in this country.' But the house is hot enough to melt cats.

Sometimes you're there in my mind's eye and then we're off. We went crabbing in Wells yesterday from that lovely harbour wall, and then we went into John's rock shop with all those colours and all that sugar turned into pink mice and pebbles and yellow lemon crystals. Do you remember that house we stayed in once in North Devon – the one with the stone statue of the girl lying on the grass? And how steep the road was down to the beach and all that light sinking into the stones and the sun through the sea mist? I loved the way nothing happened, that we just did a bit of rock pooling and looked for heart-shaped stones for Mummy. I wonder if she knows what beach they were from. I can see all those jars full of them in your kitchen.

Sometimes we would go to Mouth Mill and I would try to keep up with you as you run out of the house, down the path, over the little bridge, through the moss-covered gate and then on under the trees into the grass filled with flowers before the beach, the rocks and all that ceaseless movement.

Do you remember the summer house up on the side of the hill? There was plaster falling off the walls and some of the tiles were missing from the roof; they must have lost their grip in a storm. How still it was up there – and you noticed the difference between light and shade; and it seemed new – as if it had just been made; it had. You showed me so many things that I had forgotten about. You showed me wooden bricks and how their colours were unlike any-thing else. You showed me how timid I was at times, how unadventurous I had become – just what a fantastic feeling it is to throw butter against a wall, and to skip, and that smell and the wonderful sensation when you smudge lipstick all over your mouth.

Sometimes in the silence I can see your hands when you were babies. You had such exquisite hands, so strong for something so delicate. I remember thinking: whose hands are these? I imagined a young woman dressed in animal skins: she is walking towards a fire and she is holding you as she walks along next to a river with a group of men holding spears and children running. Then there is a man leaning against a spade; he's old now, the skin on his hands is thin and veined: he is also you at the edge of a wet field in the rain; it's evening, there is that line of gold in the distance and he picks up the spade with his hands – your hands.

I'm not really supposed to be dreaming; I'm meant to be praying. There is nothing here, not a flower, not a tree, no moss nor lichen – just rocks. The monk who usually stays in this cave showed me the shapes he had seen in the rocks: a dinosaur, a turtle and the head of a lion. I found a fossilised dinosaur claw yesterday which I will keep for you.

A couple of days ago I had a visitor called Boris: he's the chameleon I mentioned. He is not a big chameleon; he's about the length of my hand. At the moment he's greys and light browns with very light-blue spots that cover his body, and he eats the flies. I did hold up a bright pink plastic bottle next to him to see if he would change colour, but he just looked at me as if I should know better. No, he wasn't in the mood for changing and as much as I wanted him to change he was only going to do so at a time of his own choosing. I couldn't turn him pink or green or purple.

But I did try to tell him that if he became too colourful he would attract the attention of the hawks, which fly over every day at around five o'clock. They are looking for sickness and for the wounded, and they are very clever too. They can stand absolutely still and become rocks themselves. And they can become shadows, although they never cast their own. They can't see Boris; they can only see his shadow but all they are interested in is shadows. They live off shadows.

The view here is always changing. Sometimes it is like looking over a sea that God appears to have forgotten about. It's an ash-coloured sea with grey islands in it. Sometimes I don't notice the sea and can spend hours staring at the mountains, especially in the mornings. They begin to emerge out of the night as an outline as the dawn begins. The outline gradually becomes a shape; at first, it is almost black then it shifts into dark blue and changing shades of green. Before the sun arrives the mountains become purple, then pink, then red, then orange, then yellow and finally a shining gold. I never knew the desert could be so many colours all at once and all in one day. Every hour, minute and morning it is different; the colours are never the same as they were yesterday.

The nights are very quiet. Sometimes there is a little wind. But you should see the stars: it is like standing on the garage roof, watching the fireworks although there is no sound. Most of all, it is like being on the moon on your own with no one else around. And because there is no one else around my feelings have become much bigger and I don't have to think of you or imagine you: I can actually feel you flying through the air as you jump off dunes. I can hear you laughing. And when I'm feeling really lonely I just have to feel what you are doing now, like coming home from school and eating stuff out of the fridge.

There are also some sad feelings, yet it's not that you ever make me feel sad. I am sad when you are sad, and part of me wants to protect you from pain, injustice and sadness – but I can't. I will never be able to do so either. What I can do is try my hardest not to be the cause of any of those things, but I can't stop them happening. I can try my best to confront injustice and self-interest – that is the most I can do. But when you fall over, I fall over; when you are bullied, I am bullied. All I can do is try to help you deal with the sadness and the difficulties that beset us all. It is your choice as to whether you cause these or heal them.

Please try to help Mummy. I know that since we split up, life has not been easy for any of us. At the heart of why it happened was that Mummy and I felt that the model of love you were seeing was not as it should be. The way we were behaving towards one another is not how love behaves. We did try many times to mend it, but – as you know – we both needed things that the other could not give. Not because we didn't want to, but because we'd come to a point where we couldn't; because it meant trying to be somebody we were not. It meant pretending all the time, it meant not being true to ourselves, and I wanted Mummy to be true to herself and likewise she wanted the same for me. And we both wanted you to see how important that is.

So if you remember that love always turns ugliness into beauty, that's how you'll know love is real. Love enables us to be our beautiful selves, which is why it is so important. Also, we change all the time – we react like Boris – and it is through all the changes that we go through, and by noticing and feeling them continually, that we become who we are.

I can't wait to see you when I come home. I love you madly,

Daddy

Dear Prime Minister,

Have you ever been to Eastbourne after eight o'clock on a Friday night? I was there a couple of months ago with a friend. We'd gone to see a film and, walking down the High Street afterwards, it struck me that something was terribly wrong. Young men and women were being sick in the streets and in most of the doorways. There was a small group of burly men standing motionless with their hands clasped in front of them. But it was the atmosphere that struck me the most – what was being expressed in this place.

I asked myself whether I was afraid. I didn't think so: it was more an overriding sense of unease, of *dis*-ease – of the fear inherent in all of us, which had slithered so close to the surface, my friend, and I could smell it. The violence that comes from fear was barely being contained in that place. I was aware too that this was a scene that's played and replayed in most of our towns and cities on Friday and Saturday nights. But it's not your fault: I am sure every prime minister does the best they can in what must be an incredibly difficult job. No, it's as if we've all gone mad, have been driven mad and we just don't know it.

You could say it was high spirits, that night in Eastbourne – just young people having fun and so they should – but it didn't seem fun; it seemed as if they were ill. Most of them, it appeared, had money but they were spending it to quite literally 'get out of their heads' or 'off their faces'. It was both a mass bid for escape and a lament on the conditions of their captivity.

There is help for some of them, for the worst cases: counselling, methadone, safe houses. And I know you do what you can. I also know that the numbers in gaol are going up and that new prisons are being built. Of course, some of that has to do with the fact that the population of humans on this beautiful hunk of land is increasing. But some of it hasn't. Shouldn't the success of our society be measured by the fact that prisons have had to close because they're simply not needed any more? And yet time and time again, all through my life, rows of Home Secretaries have promised to build more prisons or to pay for more policemen and policewomen.

The writer and campaigner Alastair McIntosh says there is no more noble cause than bringing beauty to ugliness. Are we all suffering from a lack of beauty? Not in the sense that beauty doesn't exist but in the sense that we cannot see it any more. Is it conceivable that the job of government should be to increase instances of beauty rather than merely to seek to contain ugliness – that prisons should be places of beauty?

On that subject, I'm sure you have been to many business parks with the aim of fostering 'enterprise', which seems a strange word for creativity. Business parks look like prisons on the weekends; they even feel like prisons, where the inmates have been told there is no talking and they've been locked in their cells. Occasionally, because I'm broke most of the time, I do a day's work when it's offered to me in a business park. There, I'm surrounded by other human beings all striving for what we imagine to be a better life (which most people seem to agree is not having to strive as much whilst lapping up an exuberant standard of living).

Usually in the pre-election speeches, the phrase 'standard of living' seems to be repeated over and over again. Inherent within the phrase is the idea that those who have less should have more, and that those who have more should have even more. Encouraged by this underlying assumption, the creed of business is more, more, more – more sales, more products and, of course, more money. This raison d'être seems to be to pay as little as possible for raw materials and services, but then to charge as much as possible for making them available to everyone else, in the hopes of making more money. Some businesses go to extraordinary lengths to convince us how cheap their products are – that they are bargains – in order to tempt us to give them more of our money. But this creed of 'more' always means more for some and less for others.

The people who have the most are probably the most unwell. These people are in the unfortunate position of believing that by having more they will feel better – and for a little while perhaps they might. But it is as if they have been hypnotised and they cannot feel injustice; they seem completely unaware of the consequences of their actions, and once they have had more, they want more.

Once you are addicted to more you can never have enough.

Those who don't have more are encouraged to want it. Some of these people have to endure such damning descriptions as 'living below the poverty line' or they are labelled as something called 'poor'. Most of them may need help and some of them do get it – I know all governments try to offer what they see as help – but I am not sure they are the ones that *really* need the help. Surely the plain fact is that those with less are taking less, using less?

Whenever there is a big demonstration in the city of London, many of these people with less can be found protesting about the creed of more. I have often felt that the police are arresting the wrong people at such events – that the real damage is being done by those who are apparently respectable, not by those who are shouting and holding placards. I feel that this creed of 'more', of getting us to continually buy more and have more, is what is really leading us into catastrophe.

Over the next hundred years there will be more human beings needing more water, more food, more raw materials. Shouldn't your government be encouraging all of us to live with less, and rewarding those who do, rather than encouraging those who don't?

Three weeks ago I was walking through the eastern desert of Egypt with a group of Bedouin men. One of the many things that left an impression on me was the fact that if there was ever a catastrophe which left no food in the shops they would barely notice it. They live in harmony with their landscape in as much as the land supports them and they support it. They understood what they were looking at in the land around them: what plants were good for food, which plants were good for medicine for humans and camels. They were in relationship with their environment.

They told me the desert was becoming drier, more and more like the moon. Now, this might be a natural cycle of nature or it might not, but that's not actually the point, is it? Even if global warming isn't happening, we are still behaving as if we are insane when it comes to our relationship with the natural world. And our relationship with the natural world perfectly describes the perilous state it is in.

In the name of 'more', usually more human beings, the natural world is being ethnically cleansed. Looked at from the perspective of a butterfly or an osprey or a snow leopard, we humans are like a despotic, insecure monarch with a pathological need to suppress and control. Statements such as 'they were treated like animals' should really alarm us, because they confirm that under human dominion it is acceptable to treat animals in such an appalling manner. When the state of 'more' collapses (which it surely will) the suffering which we will all endure as a result will be nothing other than awful.

But from that abyss we will have a chance to build a new earth and form a new relationship with the natural world: one that will be based on harmony. Harmony with each other and with our environment will help us to form, inform and develop a new understanding of what being human is all about. Then, we will be able to build *with* the earth, farm *with* her, but we can only have harmony when we realise that our addiction to 'more' is what creates the disharmony within our current state of being.

You see, to adhere to the state of more, we – I – need to be in a state of almost constant agitation, essentially dissatisfied and continually craving. Surely over the generations it has been proved that continually craving more has not in fact created happiness, far from it. I have a feeling that until we place harmony at the centre of all that we strive for – all that we create – then our health service, our relationship with the environment and even our foreign policy, based as it is on the needs of the economy, can never lead to harmony. We will never find peace through striving for prosperity.

On that point, I do have something that my Bedouin brothers don't have and that is a nuclear weapon. All the young men and women in Eastbourne – they have one as well. The holders of nuclear weapons appear to be in a very powerful position because in a conflict situation our destructive power far outweighs that of those who do not possess them. Therefore it's quite natural that everyone else should want one.

Surely the present is a continual unfolding of the future, so what we do in the present moment actually describes what the next moment will be in all instances relating to ourselves?

My country (which is a notion I find increasingly unhelpful) has declared war countless times, sometimes necessarily and at other times I'm afraid just as a cover for acquiring 'more'. But have we ever in our history declared peace? I don't mean the signing of peace treaties, which invariably take place after the horror of conflict. I mean a declaration of peace. This act of declaring peace would involve giving up all our weapons of mass destruction – our bombs, our tanks, our guns – and declaring to the world that we no longer believe that killing can be morally justified. Nor can the use of violent force as a means of persuasion, as a means to get our own way and – yes – even as a means of defence, be justified.

I don't know, maybe we feel so much more than we realise. Maybe we respond to the tone of a place? In that respect, those beautiful young men and women in Eastbourne were partying like there was no tomorrow; they appeared to be doing everything in their power to forget where they were.

Up here on the moon, the planet earth shines so brightly. It is luminous – blues and greens, yellows and whites. I can sit here for hours, just looking at it, it is so beautiful.

I wish you well,

Peter

To the Girl in the Field,

I don't even know your name.

The last time I saw you I must have been about sixteen. I was walking through a field, arm in arm with Jo. We were going to a party. The grass was wet – it must have been early September – and it wasn't quite dark. You were in front of us, you turned and our eyes met. It was the first time I felt a tremor: it was as if in that moment I cracked, or you took the key from your pocket and placed it in the lock. Al once said that love between a man and a woman is like a complicated key slipping perfectly into a complicated lock.

Then you turned and carried on. That was the last time I saw you. There is not a week that goes by that I do not return to that moment, that tremor. I can still see your eyes.

There are perhaps three main types of relationships between men and women. The first is an enchantment. An enchantment is something that exists in the air; it is an attraction. We are physically attracted to so many people, sometimes just for seconds, occasionally for years and very rarely for a lifetime. An enchantment happens when we allow ourselves to dream about somebody else, to dream of intimacy.

Enchantment is a very fragile state which usually only lasts for as long as the petals stay fresh on a rose. It is the time when you inhabit my mind, when you arrive in the midst of my eating toast; when I'm looking out of the windscreen before I start the car. You inhabit the space behind thoughts. You arrive and I imagine that, in that second before we kiss – before we open our mouths – I see your lips and feel your breath and your bare shoulders; the skin beneath your shoulder blades and the warmth of your breasts on my chest; and how you would turn towards me when we are in bed . . . and, yes, how many of these enchantments are there in one lifetime? How many partners have we been to bed with, some only for seconds?

But the look in your eyes that evening went way beyond an enchantment. You looked into me, not at me.

The door beyond enchantment opens into the room of

intimacy. Intimacy is like water flowing into the details and deep soil of our being. I used to think intimacy was love. It isn't; it has within it the potential for love and it is a great teacher of love, but the teacher of Shakespeare is not Shakespeare.

Most marriages are constructed on intimacy: the willingness of two human beings to be intimate with each other emotionally, spiritually and physically. Intimacy expresses itself in the constant intention of wanting to love the other and to be loved by them. It is a state of yearning to be loved. And after a while (and that 'while' is surely different for all of us) we understand that *wanting* to love someone and *trying* to love someone means we need to put effort into that relationship. We all need to water the garden if we want anything to grow. Don't get me wrong – wanting and trying are vital, but there usually needs to be some form of compromise involved. Otherwise it is the end.

Those who compromise in this way often end up as a 'good team'. They become 'a solid pair' and they exist within the terms of their compromise, which at its best fosters a loving coexistence and deep enduring friendship. But many of these couples will begin to live with the volume turned down. They may gradually become aware of this and there can be a degree of sadness about them. Despite living with another, there is almost an air of loneliness surrounding them, which is perhaps a high price for peace.

Yet intimacy is built on trust – on the idea that we can, should we so wish, open up and reveal ourselves, entrusting our very souls to another human being. Intimacy means being brave enough to be weak. There is a wonderful line in the marriage service which says 'all that I am I give to you'. And, in time, most marriages experience this 'all', but it means all our dark as well as all our light. It is only love which can bear the darknesses and only love which heals them. When intimate relationships break down, people often use one another's weaknesses and vulnerabilities against each other, rather than attempt to heal them. There is often a great sense of betrayal that occurs when the very vulnerabilities we have entrusted to someone else are used against us. It is possibly one of the emotionally cruellest things human beings can do to each other.

When you turned around in the field – what was that, three seconds? – I know that thirty years later I can still feel it. But, really, I had no idea what lay beyond it.

More recently, I remember a morning in late summer. The bales were in the fields, I had been on the phone, and I was looking out of the window at the car that had just pulled up. It's strange, but I didn't see her until she sat down; I didn't see her until I looked into her eyes and from that moment onwards all moments have been different – the world changed, everything shifted. Suddenly I understood what everyone had been singing about; I knew at last. It was like being opened, someone laying their hands in this soil. Suddenly there was someone else in the garden and my being was not singular any more. When she left the room I could think of nothing other than her; I was amazed at her existence. I had left the earth, she had left the earth.

We met a couple of weeks later in a pub, where we sat on a bench seat next to the window. Driving back, I turned into a field full of round hay bales and we clambered up onto one. We said nothing, not a word; I could hear her breathing. I have never kissed like that before – there was no forethought, no intent, no courtship. And it's easy to say it had to happen, but there was no game-playing going on. There was no want, no desire; only energy, a current so strong.

And of course she is beautiful, but to me she was beautiful because I loved her. One of the things she taught me was how beautiful everybody else was too: the mere knowledge that all of us have that capacity to love meant that I looked at human beings completely differently from then on. And, yes, I had always believed in the theory, in the word 'love', and it is possible to discern the actions of love in history and in the acts of others. But she gave love resonance and grounding; she brought it to life – we brought it to life and it felt like taking part in eternity.

Also, I began to understand that desire in its rawest form is essentially unstable and that we are mistaken if we believe the room of desire leads to the room of love: it does not. As I said, when I met her I left the earth, stumbling around in a daze, thinking that I might wake up; that all I had to do was to blink and everything would be back to normal again and I would be returned from this wonderland. But once you have been there you can never come back, not fully.

And now the sun slides into the afternoon and the flies begin to come down from their frenzy. And, yes, in this place – in this space – there have been so many beings, but it is hers that is here and yet not here. There are times when I forget her face and the shape of her hands, but never for long. I meet her at the end of every love story. She is there when the door bell goes at home; sometimes she is arriving and I look up from where I have been planting seeds; she's there.

We saw each other for a while. I understand why I pulled away. I pulled away because I was frightened. I was frightened of the immense feelings inside me and I chose the earth, chose to return. It was the most cowardly thing I have ever done in my life.

The greatest wrong that we can commit is to deny love, to deny another human being love, to deny the chameleons and house martins love. It is the denial of love which is the root of all evil – money is simply used as the currency of denial with which we buy ourselves out of taking responsibility. This denial of love is the worst thing a human being can do. And so there I was, standing up every Sunday morning, imploring people to follow the path of love; yet when it came to it, I had neither the courage nor the integrity to do so myself. Eventually I came to my senses and called her, but I was too late. She had found someone else and they are married now.

I once met a man in a pub who showed me a book he had bought in India. Its spine had gone and I don't remember the title. The text began on white paper, but in the middle of the book there were these exquisite hand-written and illuminated sections on brown paper. Among them, there was a page that described the seven places or rooms in which we meet the divine. The first room is here in the desert, and the second room is where and when we fall in love.

I cannot buy into Alain de Botton's ice-cold reasoning that love is simply the cry of the next generation demanding to be born, a perfect fusion of complementary genes. No, that is desire – not love. Because love demands nothing of the other; love does not have a jealous grain within it. Love is not possessive; love does not demand faithfulness as its tithe. Faithfulness within relationships is something that we give to each other: it is a gift, not a price.

Maybe as we get older, the echoes that we remember – the pictures that remain – are there to teach us something. These clear images contain a truth about who we are: we face ourselves within them. The headmaster standing there, holding a cane. A time of dust in the light as I lay on the floor. The perfect poise of a damselfly landing on a leaf. Her face reflected in the moonlight we found on the other side of the tall fence, when we jumped. And the three seconds of you, real and living up here on the moon, still asking, still seeing.

What I have learned is that love is not air or water; it can never be only the one thing – it is plural. Therefore it isn't about you and me: it is always *us*. It is what the world becomes, what living becomes in the state of us; us invited into the state of love and how we grow in it, how it holds us, what it tells us, how it amazes us. We will carry on for the time being – drive our cars, answer the phone, pull crackers at Christmas – and love will carry on quietly waiting and enduring, flowing, knowing that above the floors of words and hills, we lie asleep upstairs.

Dear Osama,

We are both in a cave. Media reports on where you are (which usually demonstrate where you are not) place you in a cave somewhere on the border between Pakistan and Afghanistan. My cave is in the eastern desert of Egypt, but even here on the moon you are in the minds of monks; you are there when a mother is taking her child to school in Paris or on the subway in New York; your presence is felt on the train to work from Brighton to Victoria. There you are, coming to kill us in the name of God.

We are both sons of Adam, you a Muslim, myself a Christian. There is the one God, whom you call Allah – the one creative loving force that we both look towards. I find it strange that this one God should be leading you down your course of action and me down mine; that we are both asking for direction and receiving, it would appear, contradictory promptings, words and inspirations. Those contradictions surely centre around what it is to be righteous, a righteous child of God.

I've been reading a book recently about the English Civil War, which tore Britain apart three hundred and fifty years ago. Yes, that war had a lot of the usual root causes – the differences between those who had so much and those who had too little. But the fuel for the conflict – what drove human beings to commit acts of violence – was religion. It was the individual's belief that he or she was acting on instructions from or in the best interests of God.

As I am sure you will agree, both your religion and my religion have justified acts of violence perpetrated by the self-appointed righteous on behalf of God. This behaviour has a long fuse stretching through history and there are several examples of the Israelites behaving in the same way. More recently, of course, there was the conflict in the Balkans between different religious factions.

As one writer recently described it, the history of humanity is the history of catastrophe. Apart from natural catastrophes – meteorological and biological – most catastrophes have been the result of war. And all of those wars have been fought because men believed that they were right and on the side of right. When wars have been waged in the name of God, men and women of all faiths have believed themselves to be on the side of righteousness. In some cases, men and women have believed that their right-eous cause would eventually extend across the earth and that the domination of their particular brand of God would guarantee a lasting peace, a holy peace, God's peace. But this could not be achieved unless other human beings were characterised as a force for evil.

In much the same way as you have characterised the piece of land on which I live as being a nest of evil, the society in which I live characterises you and your followers as evil. In doing so, we are given permission to seek an end to your cause – just as you hope for an end to ours – and we are both using violent means to achieve those ends.

Even though the politicians try to persuade us other-wise, my brother, we are at war, aren't we? You and I. I am the infidel and you, you are the Moor once again. How did we end up in this position? My brother, I have never heard a list of your grievances against me. I'm sure there are many and I'm also sure many of them are justified, but I need to understand where and how I have hurt you, and what actions of mine you see as hurtful to others – not so that I can refute them, but so I can appreciate them.

I am brought food here, as I am sure you are brought food – we are both loved in that respect. These mountains, I would imagine, are very similar to the mountains where you are. Here, life exists in pockets: pockets of villages with families and livestock, children playing, gangs of crows, thirsty flies. But the largest part of it all is the cracked and creaking wilderness where grey stones gather the dust of the desert.

But is this not one land simply called by different names? Is it not one sea called by different names? And are we not one human race called by different names? Surely it is a madness to believe that the French are better than the Iranians, or that the Inuit are better than the Americans? Are we not both in this position because we somehow believe ourselves to be better than the other – to be more righteous, holier, closer to Allah than each other? Have we not accused each other of behaving in an unrighteous manner and have our actions and our beliefs not condemned each other equally? Are we both not feeding off condemnation?

In other words, we look for faults in each other which we know we will surely find, because I know they are there in me, just as you know they are there in you: they are there in all of us. And, because that is what we are concentrating on, are we not then engaged in bringing out the worst in each other? Under the spotlight of condemnation, we are both going to appear pretty awful. Worst of all, we might even convince more people to condemn each other as well – those who have never met us, who have no idea what it is to be a Muslim or a Christian. Both perspectives have nurtured some remarkable human beings and some unpalatable ones.

We can both look to scripture to justify our acts, you to the Koran and me to the New Testament. But I ask you: can God in all his goodness really be saying to you and me that we are justified in our chosen course? Would God set his beloved children against one another? Whilst our teachers may be different, their Father is the same and both look to their Father at all times.

The trouble is that both our religions apparently claim supremacy over the other, yet it doesn't feel to me as if God claims supremacy over anything. Can one act of love be more important than another? Is one birth more important than another? One tree greater than another? I feel that it is those who teach religion mainly in order to justify their own positions who have fallen into the trap of saying 'mine is better than yours'. All of which will just go to prove to those who follow neither faith that we are either insane, or that God really does hate them that much.

That is what happened in the English Civil War: both sides ended up killing each other in the name of a god they both believed in. If God is love then the carnage of a battle-field dismembers that notion completely. Love does not kill another human being; love listens, love endures, love forgives, love seeks peace and love sometimes means that we should lose our lives in defence of its being, but never that we should kill others in its name.

But this isn't about love, is it? If it were, there would at least be some hope, but at the moment there is so very little. No, it's about control or the lack of it. It's about no more than the attempt to impose our vision of freedom on each other, which is supremely arrogant on both our parts. By 'control', I mean the ability to define righteousness and

therefore control lifestyles – to impose on others our understanding of what normal is. Here, perhaps, lies the crux: you
need to be free to live your way and I need to be free to live
mine.

I know that you disapprove of my lifestyle and that you
see it as something that is corrosive to your family. For my
part, I disapprove of your lifestyle and see it as something
equally corrosive of much that I hold dear. But, as much as
they reflect who we are, our choices surely only represent
the visible part of who we have become. They are external
manifestations of the decisions we have made about what to
believe in. In isolation from each other and separated from
infatuations, erosions and corrosions, we have solidified
into Christians and Buddhists, Muslims, Hindus and Jews.
The trouble with all these perspectives is that they become
hard shells: the more certain of themselves they are, the
harder they become and the more impervious to love.

Look at creation, my brother: it moves, it is fluid,
flowing between life and death, bud, flower and seed, night
and day. In contrast, these perspectives that we both have
can hardly be described as fluid. They are fixed to the earth,
fortresses made of words. They have solidified – and are we

sure our hearts have not suffered the same fate? Once we have become solid we stop developing, we stop exploring.

Underneath the hard shells, you and I know that we are just men and that men can love each other or hate each other. But, trapped within our shells, we believe that we don't need each other and we are able to convince ourselves that we alone are right. It is a surprisingly short step from there to acting as though we have the right to impose our delusions on others.

Surely the truth is we have never been right – that you and I are merely inheritors of the traditions we have chosen? Before us there were other traditions: there were sky gods and river gods, star gods giving fertility and food; and I'm sure men and women swore by them and died for them too.

There is always the door that leads to peace. It is always open and we can walk through it any time we want. Surely, choosing to pass through it is just an individual decision that doesn't involve anyone else – it's simply our response to everyone else.

You have half the world trying to kill you, my brother, which just goes to prove how savage they really are. If they get you, you will become a martyr and the legacy of that will be more killing, more savagery and suffering. There is still time, there is always time – I hope we both die seeking peace, not waging war.

All my love,

Peter

Dear Saint Anthony,

I must admit I struggle with the notion of saints. But, having read your biography and having read what you have to say about this eternally mysterious relationship between God and human beings, there is no doubt in my mind that you reached a place – and that you continually reached for a place there in the centre of your being, your soul – where you were only ever aware of the presence of God, and how everything is held in that presence.

Your cave in the eastern desert is about a forty-five-minute walk from here, so perhaps you went this way once or twice. The birds are still here – the birds whose ancestors apparently fed you, brought you bread. They still climb in the thermals in their slow circular motion without ever moving a feather, it would seem, as they measure or *become* the current – is that the secret?

The spring from which you must have drunk has dried up and the monks who live down on the plain drive huge tankers, bringing water into the monastery you founded. The monastery couldn't exist without those deliveries.

Sometimes, if the wind is coming from the south, I can hear the monastery bell being tolled for morning and evening prayers. It's very faint though; it's as if I might have imagined it. About ten days ago I heard a donkey braying and, again, if there is a slight wind I can almost make out the whirr of a generator, but I'm not sure. As you know, this is the land of silence.

Christ said 'in my father's house there are many rooms'; this is the silent room. As you know, there are millions of others and we ourselves can inhabit thousands – there are so many to choose from. I'm quite sure the universe is full of countless billions of rooms that I can't even imagine.

Did you choose solitude or did God lead you into solitude? Or were you never truly alone, without God as your guide, your light, your companion? I know that the father of darkness kept you company and you fought what you describe as demons – spiritual physical manifestations born in darkness, hating light, which were sent to tear your being, to quite literally prevent you from praying and maintaining your relationship with God.

When I first arrived here I was afraid. I was angry that God should cast us into a world where we can become preyed upon by evil forces. How could a loving father do this – send his children out to play among forces that can tear them apart? But I have been here for several weeks now and I realise it was my choice to come here – my choice of room as it always is, as it was yours. I had been so confused and, in that confusion, weakened to the point where I blamed everyone else for the state I was in. But now I understand that I chose that state; I chose those rooms and I see now that every single action is a choice between the light and the dark.

I had thought choices were merely about survival or even about pleasure, that pleasure was a justifiable choice all of its own. In fact, the pursuit of excitement, 'kicks' and ease were all justifications for making choices. I had no idea that everything we touch – everything we are and all that we choose to experience – is actually a choice between dark and light. Nor did I understand how very sensitive we are to both those states; how with one there is the experience of increasing weightlessness while the other is heavy. Why is pleasure heavy and joy light?

Since you died some of your words have been written down. And since then many men and women have taken to the wildernesses – the quiet rooms – trying to follow your example. About sixteen hundred years ago, these men and women were almost commonplace in the land where I grew up. They, like you, took to caves and cliffs. They even built tiny cells out of reeds. There are some utterly exquisite round stone cells, more like hives, sitting on a rocky outcrop on the west coast of Ireland, there with the kittiwakes and the storm petrels inhaling the wind. But there are hardly any of us left now, hardly any in the world – perhaps no more than five hundred souls on the whole planet, living in these rooms, sleeping on stones and living on bread and dust.

In my country, it is actually against the law to live that way. If you do, you are called a vagrant. If I were to erect a small cell on Dartmoor or inhabit a fissure in the Torridon rocks, even in the far reaches of the gannet kingdom of St Kilda, or as close to the sky as I could find on Scolt Head in north Norfolk, I would be 'moved on'.

The police would be called and a pile of papers would be thrust into my hands, explaining that my actions were inappropriate and unlawful, and if I refused to go I would be forcibly arrested. Maybe somewhere in the Canadian tundra I could manage it, but apart from that I would need permission to live in the wilderness. I needed permission to come here.

There is always the moon, of course. Good and evil does not exist up here on the moon, and the silence is complete. This is a world of silence – pregnant, waiting, enduring – sometimes, I think, pleading for life. It has life in that it exists and it has landscapes and moods. I love the rooms between sunlight and dusk, when the rocks turn blue and the dust is almost silver. Sometimes I imagine it is a lake or a sea, and there are pink flamingos and fish just disturbing the surface. Yet still I crave life, idle conversation, notes of music in the distance and that noise spun by a room full of people enjoying themselves; oh, and Christmas snowmen and cakes . . . but here there is nothing, not even a breath of wind.

The food up here on the moon is passable enough, but, as my thoughts drift, the chicken tastes exactly the same as the carrots, which taste exactly the same as the chocolate cake, so I can't really taste anything any more. The water is neither hot nor cold. I have two glasses but they are the same size, so really I can't tell the difference between them. I have two sets of clothes; they too are identical.

Sometimes I imagine the shadows on the mountains are areas of heather and rising up between them are rowan and birches. I have traced streams across the contours of the rocks leading into the valleys, where there are meadows stitched with flowers, and I can hear the sound of bees . . .

And there is a woman coming towards me; with each step her eyes grow more intense and she says, 'Come, come and see what I have found'; and we walk hand in hand along a small wooded path to a gate. Through the gate there is an orchard and there are children playing, riding lions, and adults sleeping among peacocks.

Suddenly a man appears at the gate and asks, 'Are you sure you want to come through?' He looks at us closely and he goes on: 'If you do come through the gate everything you need will be provided for you, so you won't feel need any more. And as for love, there is no separation between love and hatred: it is just love. There is no desire to love, no desire to hate; there's no fear – there's just being. You can stay here as long as you want, not that you'll be aware of time any more. There is no good and evil here, so your struggle will be over. There are no decisions to make between the two because beyond this gate neither exists.'

'Is it heaven?' asks the woman.

'No, it's not heaven. We have no need of heaven. Here, heaven is another room: you go to heaven to be healed. We never get sick here; there is no such thing as pain.'

'What about pleasure?' I ask.

'No, there is joy. We are not weighed down with pleasure.'

'What about rules?' asks the woman.

'There is only one rule and if you break it you have to leave. Then you can no longer stay here.'

'Does anyone ever break it?' the woman questions.

'There was a couple, once, a long time ago, but they've gone now.' And he looks at us again.

It isn't a difficult decision. We smile and say goodbye. We walk away in silence, a little afraid I think.

EPILOGUE

Dear Father Lazarus,

It is the third week in May in southern England. Everything drips with green. I have come to realise I live in a lush land carpeted with sweet grass and now with so many colours emerging. And the sea – I can spend hours there, almost mesmerised by the way water moves light. And in the evening the gulls fly along the line of the cliffs, hauling home to a place I have no knowledge of. Maybe it's my age, but I have begun to notice that one rose is worth so much more than a bunch, and how intricate woodland is.

Father Lazarus, you said to me before I left the cave: 'Make sure, if you can, you take something back from here.' And, yes, there is a fossilised dinosaur claw on my mantelpiece and a rugged white piece of crystal that one of my

149

Bedouin brothers picked up and gave me when we were walking through the desert to St Anthony's Monastery. And for a while there was nothing else.

I returned and soon put on the weight that I had lost. And there was my pocketful of platitudes which I would trot out from time to time while leaning on the bar or after the service by the porch of whichever church I was in. I told myself I was not to revel in the experience, nor to wallow in it; that I was never to use it and increasingly I have ended up just not talking about it. But perhaps that is the most terrible of vanities.

The truth is that I am there so much of the time that the experience lies just behind the other side of the glass of normality. There were times in the cave – a lot of times – when I would sit and count the days over and over. Then, it became a massive test of will not to run. Many of my days were spent craving contact. Occasionally, I would hear a distant bell and as the dusk thickened I could see four little lights way off in the distance; just the thought that other human beings existed was so comforting.

But whilst my days were spent craving contact, the

nights were spent fearing it. Really I became a child. I remember you telling me that this wasn't going to be heaven; it was going to be hell. Without the rigorous prayer routine, six times a day for forty-five minutes, I would have ended up in a foetal position after about forty-eight hours. It wasn't necessarily the fact that prayers can lead us eventually into the arms of God; it was that they became time. They became the seasons, the leaves, the water and fields, taste and breath, and what lay within the shivering heat.

I had several long conversations with the chameleon and many short conversations with the flies (to call them unconscious beings is an unconscious act, but you know that). And I learned that even the rocks reflect rhythms, that they make different sounds at different times of the day. One of my favourite sounds was when the pigeons flew over. It happened so fast, between half past five and quarter to six in the morning. There was a small group of them, probably no more than eight birds, and yet they flew at such a speed that it sounded like the release of compressed air.

Sometimes in the evening the vultures would gather way off in the distance, circling in the golden end of the day. And once hundreds of house martins arrived late in the evening, just before it turned completely dark. They hid themselves in fissures and holes – I never saw them leave, they are such quiet birds.

I never saw the mouse you spoke about. I remember you telling me that once, when you were doing some darning, you had the chameleon on one side of you and the mouse on the other, and I wondered whether you thought they craved company. In Sussex I used to visit an elderly woman who lived on her own in a small house at the end of what was no more than a track. I would sit in the kitchen whilst she spent most of the time talking to the robins, blue tits and chaffinches who flew in and out of the kitchen doorway, landing on the table and picking up broken biscuits. I asked whether she ever felt alone and she replied, how could she, with all these friends? I now understand how completely uncomplicated that is.

I have thought about you a lot. I loved visiting your cave on the last day. It felt very different to the one you so kindly lent me, right up high at the base of that huge rock wave. Your own cave felt like more of lair, as though you were in fact slowly working your way further and further into the desert. On the other side of St Anthony's mountain, there are hundreds of miles of sand and stones that no one has ever seen, and I know you have said you want to die up there. I can see you as an older man: your black cassock is worn and weathered, and you are out there – way beyond where you are now – with your staff in your hand and your eyes the colour of sea. And you are being followed by ravens with broken wings and a collection of chameleons.

I felt it towards the end. I wasn't sure – and I'm still not – whether it is the landscape that is so intense, or whether in the absence of any life the presence of God becomes more pronounced, more palpable, and, yes, in time the gap between praying and being the prayer becomes imperceptible. You called that 'glory'. You talked about tasting 'the glory', and in that particular room of God's creation there is nothing but peace, in the sense that you have moved beyond fear of any kind and, more importantly, beyond the need of it.

I learned that fear is the worst of motivators; it feeds our shadow but we can become so adept at hiding that fact. Our craving for success, our attachment to the need for money, to respect, recognition and power – all these things – make us weak because they are so heavy and the burden of them is enormous. As a consequence we are ruled by those who are clever, but not necessarily by those who are wise.

Since I have been back I have become more aware of an undercurrent that suggests that the human race is about to enter a time of great change. Usually I am sceptical of claims that we are at the dawn of a new consciousness, but now the claims are coming from stable boys, not managing directors, from the dispossessed not the powerful. This might be the arrogance of each generation generating its own importance and conjuring eternity out of time. But it doesn't feel like that, and certainly we cannot go on as we are.

It is raining now. I can hear dripping and the vague engines of wind in the leaves.

There is something that happens to us when we are alone. We have to face the full volume of being and confront the illusion that we are completely separate. This illusion perhaps is fostered by our being physical, and, as I said at the beginning, I am now learning to move beyond observing and to understand that I am taking part in sharing something; it now feels like a sharing. This illusion of being separate has created separation. Perhaps it is when we are alone (as I am now) that we can fully appreciate what we have been parted from. The individual is a powerful illusion. While we are raindrops, we forget we are water.

The desert is the greatest teacher I have had – half mad, half real. I have returned faced with the truth that knowing ourselves is an intensely difficult thing to do, because we always seek our reflection in others. But the desert is a clear, almost unblemished, mirror. I would imagine that deep space or the surface of the moon is the same. In the desert, I could not go on making excuses and I realised how I had embedded these excuses in the fabric – in the very pattern – of my existence. I began to see how fractured we become in the mirror of materialism, just how numb it makes us.

The first of my illusions to shatter was that I was brave; you already knew I wasn't and that my attitude was merely a cover for how frightened I was, especially during the night. The second to splinter was that I liked my own company, a wretched excuse that I used to hide the fact that I was not very trusting of others – especially with my feelings – so retreat has always been the easiest option. Probably the most ridiculous illusion was that I was an 'old soul'.

I remember the afternoon after you had left me the note and the pickaxe. I wish I had kept the note; you wrote '*voilà* the pickaxe' and ended by saying 'happy step-making'. Anyway, I remember that the heat of the day was beginning to relax a little and I was sitting looking into the distance, when suddenly I saw us both as children. We were children with adult faces, but really how childish we were, how fragile and stubborn, as we traced the shapes of animals in rocks and talked to the birds. And yet it was such a release to know that we are not old; we are new. We are new creations at the mercy of love, desire, beauty and fear, trying to compress each second into order and reason.

Yes, there is the mirror of order and the mirror of reason, but if that is all we see reflected of ourselves, then in time we will become an interesting collection of molecules and no more. Not that there is anything wrong with that; maybe such a view of ourselves would mean that we'd take responsibility for our own creations rather than handing fate and love and pain over to God, and sex and money to the devil. No, up here on the moon we know we are using order merely as threads to tie us to the surface, to reach the doorway to eternity. But that's our choice, isn't it?

Richard Dawkins has simply made other choices, and I can quite understand why he should feel aggrieved at being condemned to a hell he does not believe in. The idea of hell is really an old-fashioned curse. All the same, I have no wish to be condemned as a lunatic because of what the universe has told me, or because I feel life is a gift rather than an accident. Listening to the two sides spar – believer and non-believer – is rather like overhearing a conversation between a chaffinch and a mackerel, one trying to bend reason into faith, the other trying to bend faith into reason.

Since I have been back I think about you almost every day. You are here making coffee, or walking in the distance – a lone figure in all that heat, in those big boots with metal toecaps. I know that in some senses it was pain that brought you to the desert, the pain of loss. But you have been water to so many lives with your humility and your humour. And you are still there, struggling and praying and being born, coming alive. You were able to cut through all the clutter that I brought with me and to go straight to the mirror of my being.

I found that being in the desert intensified so much of what I saw and it became so utterly beautiful, especially during the beginnings and the ends of the day. Maybe it was because I was seeing it for the first time, but it felt like seeing it as it really is. Maybe that is resurrection, the seed opening?

As I get older the world seems to be becoming more vivid, more extraordinary, and, as I said at the beginning, I'm not observing it any more: now it feels like sharing. I am not something separated from it any longer and that sense of being has come back with me. Last week I was driving to a small festival in Sussex. The leaves were new and they spread, almost floating, above the road; and the sight and the light were so intense I had to stop the car because I was crying so much.

In reality it is all one: the desert is one with water, and water is one with bone, and bone is one with sound; there is no separation. And when I understood this I began to realise the 'I' that I perceive is made up of so many different people: their reflection in me, my reflection in them and that this process is ongoing. There is no such thing as 'my' life in isolation. We are to a large extent reflective surfaces onto which some experience settles and, to an even greater extent, we are made who we are by those around us, whom we have become one with – those who have opened us, stilled us, horrified us and dared to love us. They have been our spiritual directors. In this way, we are all part of a moving image, a living image; we are all continually formed and reformed in all that we meet, all we love, all that is broken by doubt and insecurity, by knowing love and aloneness. Being made in the image of God means we are all connected. As T. S. Eliot says, 'the rose and the stone are one'.

During the time I spent in your cave, I learned that separateness is a very powerful illusion; that individualism has been a terrible distortion of who we are. Our cult of individualism was born, I sense, out of the loneliness that crept into us when we disconnected ourselves from the land and aimed for bigger and bigger houses with higher and higher walls. It is when we disconnect from the land, from the sea, from ants and house martins, from pain and love – when we do not see our own reflection in all life, in each other – that we become marooned, isolated and fearful.

And in the desert I learned that life is precarious. We human beings can choose comfort if we wish, to crave luxury; luxury is so cold. Until we choose the precarious – face it, feel it, every sixteen pounds per square inch, the imperceptible floating of this little ball in the middle of nothing, the fabulous space beyond us, in front of us and behind us – we can never feel what it is to live. What makes us different is that we can know our vulnerability and it is only when we know it – know our living, know our death – that we can recognise our aloneness. And when we recognise our aloneness, only then can we under-stand our togetherness, with the wonderful chaos and tenderness that brings.

God, I loved the desert. It allowed me to see to what was

broken – with all my hate, with all my love, my unknowing, my unbeing – and gave me the time to begin to mend. And I understood that I am a collection of everything that has ever happened – everything that was chosen, rejected, valued, recognised. And in that sense I began to see how much we all owe the chameleon, the vultures and the house martins, God, the sky and the fossils, the light and the shade, the men and the women. For without their reflection we are pale and languid.

I wish you well, Lazarus, and thank you for lending me your cave. I will return one day.

All my love,

Peter